About the author

Andrew Lockhart-Mirams is a Solicitor, Senior Partner of Lockharts Solicitors and Fellow of the Institute of Chartered Arbitrators. He has specialised in NHS regulatory law and the law affecting General Practitioners for many years. In this book he examines and explains the wide range of legal issues which affect general practice today.

Acknowledgments

To my colleagues Rosalind Parkin and Harjit Lidder without whom the completion of this book would not have been possible.

Andrew Lockhart-Mirams

Foreword

The rapidity of change of general practice within the UK during the past decade has been paralleled by the increasing quality and quantity of legal issues affecting primary care. The past decades of a fairly low level of legal actions brought against doctors and their staff has been replaced by a litigation-minded society where the threats of legal action against practitioners has become an almost daily occurrence. Thus today's GP may find himself at odds with the law for a variety of reasons.

We are all aware of the increasing number of complaints being brought against general practices in Industrial & Employment Tribunals across the country. The implications of the employment laws are there to be understood by individual practitioners and their managers if we are to avoid unnecessary, and often acrimonious, disputes between our employees and us.

We are all aware that with the increase of information sources available more patients are readily taken action against their doctors through either formal complaints procedures, via regulatory authorities, or by direct legal action against the doctor. Perceived patient mismanagement is something we can only protect against by being continually 'on guard' against a variety of risk factors. One of these is confidentiality. Ever an issue in general practice, it is now becoming more difficult to guard against confidential leakages of information with increasing demands for information from employers, the police and other external agencies. The management of patient personal data has been the subject of GMC advisory booklets and the Data Protection Act 1998 and its cardinal eight principles.

At the end of the day, no doctor can be a lawyer but he/she can be more aware of the legal issues affecting their practice. A little more than a basic understanding of the law is necessary in today's medical practice. The basic information required to run regular and appropriate risk evaluation and management programmes in primary care can often help to avoid adverse situations and their attendant possible legal outcomes. Due diligence is a constant necessity.

In this concise volume 'A Guide to Law in General Practice', Andrew Lockhart-Mirams manages to take the legal issues affecting general practice today and adroitly explains the background, at the same time crystallising the practical implications for practitioners and their practices. All the current models are there from 'the Caldicott Guardians' to 'NHS Zero Tolerance to Violence'. This is a book which is easy to read, well set-out and a useful book for the general practitioner.

Dr Morris Pearlgood

Consultant Medical Advisor in Primary Care
SE London

Applicable Law

The law in this book is stated as at the 1 November 2001. The Law as stated applies to General Practitioners working in England. In some areas, such as the application of the Medical Act 1983 (which deals with, amongst other things, the establishment of the General Medical Council), the stated provisions apply additionally throughout Scotland, Wales and Northern Ireland. Although considerable efforts have been made to state the relevant law as at the 1 November 2001, the statements of necessity can be no more than a summary of the many provisions covered and in all jurisdictions GPs should check with their professional advisor, the British Medical Association or their Medical Defence Organisation before proceeding.

CONTENTS

INTRODUCTION

The law and its origins

The United Kingdom is a country rich in law. The standard summary of English Law (Hailsbury's Laws of England) is about 60,000 pages long and although very detailed, is still only a summary. There are multitudes of Acts of Parliament which date back to the 19th Century and beyond, and many of the provisions only relate to England. Printed Acts of Parliament are supplemented by a massive bulk of Statutory Instruments which, in many cases again, only relate to England. In Scotland and in Northern Ireland the Law is in many respects different and, since the establishment of the Welsh Assembly, there is an increasing volume of law applicable only to Wales. The Channel Islands and the Isle of Man also have their own individual legal systems.

In practice, whilst the various systems are to a greater or lesser extent similar, the difference is in the detail. Obviously no individual could possibly "know" any more than a tiny fragment of the law; nor does anyone need to know the entire law. Lawyers usually know quite a lot about one particular area of the law together with a general understanding of a much wider framework. Possibly one of the most important aspects of lawyers' training is how to research an answer either directly from the Statute Law or with the assistance of a standard text such as *Hailsbury's Laws of England*.

Law is derived from a variety of different sources. The most basic is "Customary Law" which consists of the accepted rules of society. As society develops and has new needs, it adds new laws to the system and old laws fall away. In English law, these rights and rules are the original basis for the Criminal Law and the Law of Tort (which deals, for example, with compensation after an accident). Another source of law which has grown up over the centuries is the Law of Contract; for example, the terms by which merchants buy and sell and the terms of contract dealing with the provision of services – a type of contract of particular relevance to the provision of Personal Medical Services (PMS) under the National Health Service (Primary Care) Act 1997.

Over time these various laws have formed the mass of English law known as "Common Law" which consists of the decisions that Judges have made in past cases which have come before the Court, and which have transformed Customary Law into "Judge-made Law".

The system of Common Law, even though it does allow the law to evolve, is not however adequate to deal with the sort of complex society which has developed in the UK. For the past 800 years this process of conscious invention of law has been done by the Monarch in Council and then by Parliament and is called Legislation or Statute Law. Statute Law requires Parliament to pass laws (Statutes) or give limited law-making powers to Ministers and others who can then make the law (including statutory instruments, regulations, byelaws etc). The system of Statute Law and Common Law run side-by-side but, the two come closer together when there is doubt on the correct interpretation and meaning of Statute Law and Judges are required to make and pronounce the final decision.

From the Middle Ages to the end of the 19th Century there were two systems of Court running in parallel. In addition to the Courts that enforced Common Law and Statute Law, there was a system of Courts of Conscience – the "Courts of Equity". These could in certain cases intervene to enforce principles of fairness and they supplemented the Common Law and prevent injustice. These Courts of Equity developed the earliest laws of confidentiality and of wills and trusts. Now all Civil Courts apply both Common Law and Equity.

In 1973 the United Kingdom joined the various organisations now known as the European Union. As a result, the UK is now part of a larger society in which an increasing amount of law-making is done on a European basis rather than simply for the UK, or for one of the Constituent Countries.

The law in general practice

General practice is subject to the same body of laws as the rest of society. The volume of law which potentially has an impact both on General Practitioners, and those who work for them, is therefore considerable. However, the purpose of this book is to provide an outline guide to those areas of law which have a day to day significance to General Practitioners.

The law covered is from all the main sources discussed above and more. Whilst most of it is of general applicability, some of it relates only to general practice – for example specific provisions of the regulations under which NHS general practice is provided. Other aspects of law, for example the duty of confidentiality or questions of health and safety at work, while being common to all business relationships, are of greater importance in a clinical setting and have aspects which are unique.

CHAPTER 1

GENERAL PRACTICE AND THE NATIONAL HEALTH SERVICE

The legal framework of general practice

The National Health Service (NHS) was brought into existence by the NHS Act 1946. Since, then there has been a continual process of change and development and frequent Acts of Parliament to implement new arrangements. Most of the key provisions in Statute Law relating to the Health Service are contained in the NHS Act 1977 (and its Scottish and Northern Irish equivalents), the NHS and Community Care Act 1990, the NHS (Primary Care) Act 1997, the Health Act 1999, and the Health and Social Care Act 2001

Section 1 of the NHS Act 1977 requires the Secretary of State to continue the promotion of a comprehensive health service designed to secure improvement in the health of the people, and in the prevention, diagnosis and treatment of illness.

Prior to the coming into force of the NHS (Primary Care) Act 1997, the contractual basis of the General Practitioners contract was set out in Section 29(1) of the NHS Act 1977, which, as enacted, provides:

> "It is every Area Health Authority's duty, in accordance with regulations, to arrange as respects their area with medical practitioners to provide personal medical services for all persons in the area who wish to take advantage of the arrangement. The services so provided are in this Act referred to as 'General Medical Services'".

Section 29(2), further stipulated that regulations may define the Personal Medical Services (PMS) to be provided and ensure that the arrangements will be such that all persons availing themselves of those services will receive adequate personal care and attendance.

Whilst the title "Area Health Authority" has changed over the period of time to "Health Authority", the provisions of Section 29(1) remain the bedrock upon which traditional GP services are provided. Section 29 is found at the start of Part II of the 1977 Act and the services that are provided are often referred to as "Part II Services".

The regulations referred to in Section 29(2) are set out in the NHS (General Medical Services) Regulations 1992 as amended and the Terms of Service for Part II General Practitioners are contained in Schedule 2 of these regulations. The regulations have been negotiated over many years between the Department of Health and the General Practitioners Committee of the British Medical Association (BMA), formerly the General Medical Services Committee. The regulations are the framework within which Part II General Practitioners work. They determine how a doctor may be permitted to practise in the area, what their terms for service are and how they are paid. Payments are made in accordance with the Statement of Fees and Allowances (commonly known as the "Red Book") published by the Secretary of State.

With effect from 1 April 1998 however, an alternative type of GP contract came into existence. This was when Pilot Schemes for the provision of Personal Medical Services (PMS), as opposed to General Medical Services were introduced in accordance with the NHS (Primary Care) Act 1997.

The services that are to be provided under a Pilot Scheme, are set out in an agreement made between the commissioner of the services and the provider of the services. Although such agreements may incorporate some of the regulatory provisions contained in the Part II framework, they are locally negotiated agreements between the parties for the provision of services. This arrangement can be contrasted with the statutory nature of the Part II GP Contract.

The provisions of the NHS (Primary Care) Act 1997 are supported by a regulatory framework set out in statutory instruments and directions, which provide that, although the contracts can contain local elements, the provision of basic practitioner services, in so far as they are provided to patients, are the same under both the Pilot Schemes and Part II arrangements.

A specific note about PMS contractual obligations and pilot schemes is set out at the end of this chapter

NHS General Practitioners' obligations to patients (Terms of Service)

At any time, a General Practitioner has a list of patients, which is kept by the Health Authority (HA) and apart from those treated under temporary or emergency arrangements, these are the patients for whom they are responsible. These patients are those people who have chosen to be treated by that GP and have been accepted onto the list, or who have been allocated to the GP by the HA. Where a GP accepts a patient or removes one from the list, it is important that the HA is notified as soon as possible so that there is no uncertainty as to who is, and who is not, a patient.

Although NHS general practice is the subject of much law and regulation, there is no actual definition of general practice. Paragraph 12 of the Terms of Service states that:

"A doctor shall render to his patients all necessary and appropriate medical services of the type usually provided by general medical practitioners."

The failure to define 'appropriate medical services' reflects the complexity and changing nature of general practice. In effect, it implies that "general practice is what General Practitioners do". This definition emphasises the importance of the regulation of the profession by the profession. An individual doctor can in theory be in breach of their Terms of Service if they fail to deliver the services which their colleagues provide. It is a modern example of what was discussed in the Introduction – the law giving effect to the established and accepted customs of society.

However, while the Terms of Service do contain this all-embracing statement, they also list many specific duties, which a GP is obliged to perform:

1   Give general advice, where appropriate, on the patient's general health and in particular about the significance of diet, exercise, the use of tobacco, the consumption of alcohol and the misuse of drugs and solvents.

2   Offer patients consultations, and, where appropriate, physical examinations for the purpose of identifying, or reducing the risk of, disease and injury.

3   Offer, and where appropriate, provide vaccination or immunisation against measles, mumps, rubella, pertussis, poliomyelitis, diphtheria and tetanus.

4   Make appropriate referrals for the provision of any other services under the NHS Act.

5   Give advice as appropriate to enable patients to avail themselves of services provided by a local social services authority.

In addition, PMS contractors are required by the Implementation Directions relating to Pilot Schemes, to provide an adequate cervical smear test upon request to all patients who are women aged between 25 and 64 (who have a cervix) at intervals of no more than five-and-a-half years, and at such shorter intervals as may be appropriate, to all patients for whom the need for a cervical smear test is indicated by the result of a previous test or other treatment

As well as the core requirements set out above, the Terms of Service also require, amongst other things, that GPs offer a health check to elderly patients, and provide a health check for new patients or patients not seen within three years if requested. GPs must also provide, free of charge, a number of specified certificates and provide drugs and appliances that are needed for the treatment of any patient to whom they are providing services.

A Part II GP is responsible for ensuring that the services referred to in Paragraph 12 are provided to his patients throughout each day that their names appear on the Medical List. The obligation on Pilot Scheme providers is put slightly differently in that the provision of PMS has to be available throughout each 24-hour period that the scheme is in existence. Part II GPs have to comply with specific availability requirements but these have not been carried across into the mandatory part of Pilot Schemes.

GPs do not, however, have to provide every service personally, but, they do have to be satisfied that where services are provided by a deputy or another person, such persons are appropriately qualified and competent to discharge the duties that they are required to undertake.

Appropriately qualified GPs may also provide other services to patients – child health surveillance, contraceptive services, maternity medical services or minor surgery – and in each case the HA, or the commissioning body in the case of Pilot doctors, has to be satisfied that the GP has the necessary experience and competence and, where appropriate, is working from properly equipped premises; for example in the case of minor surgery services.

In providing any of these services, whether under Part II or a Pilot Scheme, a GP is clearly under a duty to provide a good service. In doing so, they must not act negligently. This means that they must act with the care, skill and diligence appropriate to a reasonable GP. A doctor does not guarantee the result of treatment; simply because treatment is unsuccessful does not mean that the doctor has failed to do the job properly. A doctor is not guilty of negligence if they have acted in accordance with a practice accepted as correct by a responsible body of medical practitioners skilled in that particular form of treatment, even if there is another body of opinion opposed to that practice. Clearly, no doctor can be an expert in every aspect of clinical practice. A GP is expected to be competent at general practice, and if they provide additional services, they should provide them competently. The standard to which services are to be provided is set out in Paragraph 3 of the Terms of Service:

> *"Where a decision whether any, and if so what, action is to be taken under these Terms of Service requires the exercise of professional judgement, a doctor shall not, in reaching that decision, be expected to exercise a higher degree of skill, knowledge and care than:*
>
> *(a) in the case of a doctor providing child health surveillance services under Regulation 28, maternity medical services under Regulation 31, or minor surgery services under Regulation 33, which any general practitioner included in the child health surveillance list, the obstetric list or, as the case may be, the minor surgery list may reasonably be expected to exercise; and*
>
> *(b) in any other case, that which general practitioners as a class may reasonably be expected to exercise."*

A comparable provision applies to Pilot Scheme contractors.

This statutory definition of what is an acceptable standard of care is therefore a re-statement of the duty of care that doctors owe to their patients in the Tort of Negligence, and they must always use the level of skill which is expected of GPs. A failure to meet this standard, which causes harm to a patient, exposes the GP to the risk of a claim for damages or, in very extreme circumstances, to a prosecution for manslaughter.

General Practitioners' responsibilities to staff

Although the major issues of GP/staff relations are dealt with in later chapters, the Terms of Service do lay certain specific responsibilities on GPs with respect to their staff.

Paragraph 17 of the Terms of Service for Part II GPs requires doctors to treat patients who attend during surgery hours. If an appointments system operates and a patient attends without an appointment, then the doctor may refuse to see the patient then and there. However, the patient has to be offered a reasonable appointment and the patient's health must not be put in danger, in addition:

> "a doctor shall take reasonable steps to ensure that no refusal is made without his knowledge".

In order for a doctor to be able to do this, good and effective communication between the staff and the GP is essential. The requirements of this paragraph have not been carried across into Pilot Scheme Agreements.

Paragraph 28 obliges Part II GPs, before taking on any member of staff, to make sure that the individual is suitably qualified and competent to do the job. It also requires them to give all employees opportunities for training to maintain their competence. A similar provision applies to Pilot Schemes.

The training and competence of a GP's employees is of crucial significance to the GP for many obvious reasons. An employer is responsible in law for the actions of an employee under the principle of Vicarious Liability. A GP will almost always be held responsible in law if something goes wrong in the care of a patient resulting from a failure by one of his employees. This could mean a claim for damages, a disciplinary committee hearing or conduct proceedings before the General Medical Council (GMC).

Personal Medical Services contractual obligations

As noted above, from 1 April 1998, an alternative type of GP Contract was introduced under the provisions of the NHS (Primary Care) Act 1997. The Act provides for the establishment of both Pilot Schemes and Permanent Arrangements under Part II of the NHS Act 1977. At present however, no Permanent Arrangements have been set up in England, although, it is clear from the NHS Plan that Permanent Arrangements will be introduced in due course.

Personal Medical Services (PMS) Pilots, the first of which commenced in April 1998, were introduced to explore different ways of contracting so as to address local service issues and pilot new ways of delivering and improving services. Various aims have been set out, including addressing recruitment and retention problems, reducing bureaucracy, providing more flexible employment opportunities together with opportunities and incentives for Primary Care Professionals to use their skills to the full. It is however the case that, most, if not all, of these aims would be attainable by Part II GPs. In this regard particular reference is made to the availability within Part II of funding for local development schemes under Section 36 of the NHS (Primary Care) Act 1997. The schemes provide a mechanism whereby money can be transferred from the Hospital and Community Health Services budget into primary care. The monies are intended to pay for an enhancement in medical services. Examples include:

1   Disease management programmes where a practice might enhance its usual services to patients who have medical conditions (such as epilepsy) which are not covered by the existing national contract but are key priorities in a local strategy

2   Enhancing General Medical Services where funding might pay for dedicated nursing time to encourage women to have cervical smears

3   Providing workforce flexibilities such as employing an assistant to free up GPs for training time

4   For the employment of a counsellor or a skilled therapist to deal with mental health problems. Funding is at the discretion of the Health Authority in consultation with the Local Medical Committee. Such schemes are not however available to Pilot Scheme doctors working under Part I and the flexibility which Section 36 Schemes provided is now to be incorporated in the Pilot Scheme Agreement.

Pilot Scheme Agreements are locally negotiated contracts; an arrangement on which the Department of Health has placed considerable emphasis. However, in reality, all Pilot Scheme Agreements are subject to a considerable National Regulatory Framework contained particularly in the implementation directions, the Health Authorities and Primary Care Trusts Implementation of Pilot Schemes (Personal Medical Services) Directions 2001 and through a "National Core" document introduced in October 2000: *"A contractual framework for personal medical services – the third wave pilots"*.

The implementation directions carry across into Pilot Schemes many of the provisions that are contained in a Part II GP's Terms of Service. Accordingly, the areas where there is room for local negotiation are limited; in the main to the provision to the particular services and to particular arrangements for the collection and monitoring of information about the delivery of healthcare.

Two types of Pilot Scheme Contracts are possible. PMS Contracts, where the only services provided are those which the patient would expect to receive from a Part II GP together with, if agreed, maternity medical services, minor surgery services and contraceptive services. An enlarged form of PMS Contract provides for the above services together with the provision of identified non-GMS services.

All income and expenses received by a Pilot Scheme Doctor are cash limited, in that an annual contract price (subject to permitted variations) is agreed at the outset and no additional payments are made even if costs increase, and are subject to local renegotiation. This differs remarkably from the arrangements for Part II GPs where all income and all direct expenses are non-cash limited. For example, unless covered by an exemption, Part II GP remuneration is not limited by an overall figure and the Secretary of State is under a duty to pay to each Health Authority the cost of such remuneration and cannot impose a ceiling thereon. Similarly certain items of expenditure, such as surgery rent and rates are directly and fully reimbursed. Conversley however cash limits are imposed, for example, on the reimbursement of salary costs.

Although the position is not free from doubt, it is generally accepted that Part II GPs work in accordance with the provisions of a statutory contract, the terms of which can, subject to consultation between the Department of Health and representatives of the profession, be changed unilaterally. A Pilot Scheme Agreement is a contract for the provision of services and whilst changes can be imposed through alterations to the implementation directions, the locally negotiated elements can only be varied with the consent of both parties.

There are a large number of differences between the Part II arrangement and a Pilot Scheme Agreement. Many of the differences are ones which doctors intending to move into a Pilot Scheme will discuss with professional advisors, but some of the major differences are identified below:

1 Subject to Professional Conduct issues and what might broadly be described as "good behaviour", a Part II Contract is available to a GP up until the compulsory retirement age of 70. A Pilot Scheme Agreement is unlikely to be written for a term of more than three years and there is no information available at present as to the arrangement, which will be made when Pilot Schemes become permanent.

2 On moving to a Pilot Scheme, GPs leave the medical list, although, in the majority of cases, they will benefit from a preferential right of return if they wish to move back to provide Part II services. A new doctor, however, starting work in a Pilot Scheme will not be able to move into Part II work unless certain specific criteria can be satisfied.

3 Whilst an overall responsibility to provide services applies both to Part II and Pilot Schemes, there are no specific availability requirements that apply to Pilot Schemes.

4 A Part II GP's remuneration is calculated in accordance with the Statement of Fees and Allowances. Both Capitation Payments and Item of Service Payments are very work-sensitive in that the more patients you have and the more items of service, such as night visit fees, you carry out, the more you get paid. A Pilot Scheme doctor is paid in accordance with the provisions of the Contract, many of which, for example, only provide for basic price increases where there is a variation in patient list size of more than plus or minus 2% or even as much as plus or minus 5%.

5   Whilst Part II GPs can depend on their nationally negotiated contract and on nationally negotiated provisions for the reimbursement of expenses, (such as premises costs, including items such as improvement grants and computer costs), Pilot Scheme doctors have to ensure that appropriate provisions are specifically included in their contracts.

6   Although not applicable to Wave I and Wave II Pilot Schemes, GPs now entering Pilot Schemes are required to give six months notice to terminate the scheme whereas, Part II contractors only have to give three months notice to resign from the medical list.

7   Arrangements for discipline are different. The Discipline Committee procedures do not apply to Pilot Schemes, but Pilot Scheme Contracts will contain specific provisions as to how defaults are to be dealt with.

8   Superannuation arrangements for Pilot Scheme GPs should certainly be no less favourable than they are for Part II Contractors, but specific arrangements to provide for this need should be contained in the Pilot Scheme Agreements. Detailed arrangements however for superannuation are still to be clarified.

9   Through the National Core Contract Pilot Scheme, providers are required to comply with National Service Frameworks, Health Improvement Plans, Cancer Guidelines, Clinical Governance and the provision of Professional Development Plans. Such requirements do not presently apply to Part II Contractors.

10 The National Core Contract for Pilot Schemes provides that patients should be able to see a Primary Care Professional within 24 hours and a GP within 48 hours where care is provided either by the Pilot itself or by entering into an arrangement with another

practice or a walk-in centre. It is expected that this target should be achieved by 2002 and must be achieved by 2004. Access is not a concept which appears in the Terms of Service for Part II practitioners, but the practitioner's responsibility to patients extends beyond the 24-hour period whether it is discharged personally, or by a deputy or assistant acting on their behalf. Specifically however, a doctor has to be available for specific periods and, subject to certain exceptions, doctors have to be available for 42 weeks in any period of 12 months, for not less than the number of hours specified in any Medical Practice Committee determination and on five days in any such week. The hours for which a doctor will normally be available in any week being allocated between the days on which he will normally be available in that week and in such manner as is likely to be convenient to his patients. In determining availability, account may be taken of any period when the doctor is attending at his practice premises or at any clinic provided by him for his patients and of any time spent making domiciliary visits. No account however can be taken of time spent by the doctor holding himself in readiness to make domiciliary visits.

11 The financial arrangements for Part II GPs are governed by the Statement of Fees and Allowances and monitored through post-verification checks. All the financial provisions for a Pilot Scheme are set out in individual contracts and many Health Authorities have sought to impose onerous and extensive provisions.

The above list is by no means an exhaustive list of the differences between Part II Contracts and Pilot Schemes, but it serves to demonstrate the fundamentally different nature of a General Medical Services Contract and a Pilot Scheme Agreement.

A General Practitioner's obligation to his Partners

Although this book does not attempt to cover in any detail the multitude of Partnership Arrangements that can be made between GPs, whether Part II contractors or doctors performing Personal Medical Services, it is the case that increasingly Health Authorities and Primary Care Trusts are recognising GP Practice arrangements as practice-based rather than a series of individual contracts entered into between the GP and the relevant authority. Apart from the reasons set out below, this trend is in itself a reason for GPs to have formalised practice arrangements so that everyone in the Partnership is co-ordinated in the discharge of their obligations to the commissioning authority.

What is not understood by many doctors is that if they have no Partnership Deed, the law contained in the Partnership Act 1890 governs the arrangements between the Partners and, whilst a basic framework for a Partnership Arrangement is provided, there are many consequences which are extremely unsatisfactory in general practice. These consequences include the following:

- Unless otherwise agreed the Partners share the profits (and losses) of the partnership equally

- All Partners must have free access to the Partnership bank account and are entitled to take part in managing the business

- Partnership decisions may be made by a majority of the Partners except that all Partners must consent to a new Partner being admitted as well as any change in the nature of the business

- All Partners are regarded as agents of the Partnership and can make commitments which bind all the other members of the Partnership

- Partners must not compete with the business of the Partnership and if they engage in any business on their own account in the same field of activity any income therefrom must be paid to the Partnership

- All Partners are jointly and severally liable for the acts and omissions of the Partnership and for the acts of individual Partners carried out during the course of the Partnership

- The Partnership ends automatically on the death, retirement or bankruptcy of one of the Partners

- No Partner can be expelled from the Partnership

- Any Partner can choose to end the Partnership at any time on giving notice to the other Partners

- At the end of the Partnership there are no restrictive covenants

- When the Partnership ends there will be an automatic termination of the contracts of all the Partnership employees and unless they are re-engaged by the Partners who elect to continue in the business they may pursue a claim for redundancy

- If the Partnership ends, all the Partners are left with their own patient lists although a former Partner has no automatic right to take the patients on the list with him

- Each Partner is, in general, entitled to force a sale of the Partnership assets, which are capable of being sold, and to have the value of any unsaleable assets bought into account by the Partner who retains it.

Although there are no statistics available, it is believed by many Local Medical Committee secretaries that only some 50 or 60% of Partnerships are governed by a current Partnership Deed. Certainly, as suggested, the lack of properly regulated Partnerships is a cause for concern and in some areas Health Authorities/Primary Care Trusts are specifically requiring that those who enter into Pilot Schemes have a formalised Partnership Deed.

The arrangements that would be covered in a formal Deed are many and varied but certainly, at a minimum, Partners will wish to consider provisions relating to:

- Surgery premises

- Partnership capital

- Partnership bank accounts

- The definition of Partnership earnings and individual earnings of the Partners

- What are to be Partnership expenses and Partners' individual expenses

- Superannuation arrangements

- Authorised leave from the practice including: holiday leave, continuing medical education leave, absence due to illness, maternity, paternity, adoption, compassionate and extended leave and service in the Armed Forces

- The Partners' obligations to each other together with a list of the restrictions that apply to the actions and authority of Partners

- Voting and arbitration provisions

- Mutual assessment periods for any new Partners

- Provisions relating to voluntary retirement

- Provisions relating to expulsion from the practice

- Arrangements to deal with concerns about fitness to practise

- The effect of retirement together with the provisions for the purchase of a retired Partner's share in the business

- Restrictive covenants

- Provisions regarding the president Partner who is required to sign the Partnership tax return

- How notices are to be served and

- Various other standard clauses to facilitate the running of the Partnership.

Despite the clear advantages of having Partnership Deeds many practices throw away the protection afforded. This is because they do not realise the ramifications when they admit new Partners, and this includes Partners admitted subject to a period of mutual assessment. The effect of this is that the provisions of the existing Deed become null and void unless either there is a new Partnership Deed, or a Deed of Variation and Accession, in place before the new Partner starts, or in the case of the new Partner and the continuing Partners specifically agreeing that they are bound by the terms of the existing Partnership Deed unless otherwise stated in writing between the Partners.

CHAPTER 2

MEDICAL AND NURSING ETHICS

Medical ethics

Medicine is a profession and, as such, it requires a prolonged period of training as well as mental ability. Professionals are expected to abide by high standards for their own sake, especially in respect of confidentiality (Chapter 3). They also owe a wider duty to the community, which may conflict with their duty to a particular patient. Doctors have to be registered with the General Medical Council (GMC), which sets standards for the profession on questions of conduct and ethics. Through their special knowledge, training and responsibilities, doctors are in a position of considerable power and influence with regard to their patients.

Hand-in-hand with the responsibility of being a member of a profession, there is the obligation to behave in accordance with professional standards. All professions (doctors, lawyers, accountants, engineers etc.) lay down codes of conduct to which members of the profession are expected to adhere. One of the key responsibilities of a profession, is to ensure that such codes are respected by their members; if they are not, then it is the profession's obligation to discipline and even, on occasion, to withdraw the right of an individual to practise. This chapter considers broad questions of ethics. In the next chapter consideration is given to some specific problem areas.

The first code of conduct for doctors dates back about 4,000 years and the Hippocratic Oath dates back about 2,500 years. There have been numerous other codes drafted since then. Many of the provisions of the codes seem strange to modern eyes, although there are some matters in old codes which are strikingly familiar:

> *"I will not cut for stone, even for patients in whom the disease is manifest; I will leave this operation to be performed by practitioners."*

This stark demarcation between medicine and surgery reflected and influenced a division which continued for nearly all recorded history and (in a more benign form) still has influence. However, fundamental principles enunciated by Hippocrates still resonate:

> *"I will prescribe regimen for the good of my patients according to my ability and my judgement and never do harm to anyone. To please no one will I prescribe a deadly drug, nor give advice which may cause his death. All that may come to my knowledge in the exercise of my profession or outside of my profession or in daily commerce with men, which ought not to be spread abroad, I will keep secret and will never reveal."*

Since the Second World War and the concern about the activities of some doctors under the Nazis, there has been an international code of ethics, the Declaration of Geneva, for doctors.

The Declaration of Geneva states:

- I solemnly pledge myself to consecrate my life to the service of humanity

- I will give to my teachers the respect and gratitude which is their due

- I will practise my profession with conscience and dignity

- The health of my patient will be my first consideration

- I will respect the secrets which are confided in me, even after the patient has died

- I will maintain by all means in my power, the honour and the noble traditions of the medical profession

- My colleagues will be my sisters and brothers

- I will not permit considerations of age, disease or disability, creed, ethnic origin, gender, nationality, political affiliation, race, sexual orientation or social standing to intervene between my duty and my patient

- I will maintain the utmost respect for human life from its beginning even under threat and I will not use my medical knowledge contrary to the laws of humanity

- I make these promises solemnly, freely and upon my honour.

(World Medical Association, 1948, as subsequently amended)

It is not possible to make a full and exhaustive statement that entirely describes or defines medical ethics. Medical ethics are constantly evolving in response to the pressures of society and the thinking of doctors. For example, the Geneva Declaration, as drafted in 1948, clearly no longer reflects contemporary attitudes to abortion. Some argue that, whatever the ethical rules may be, there will always be circumstances in which, while the letter of the law is obeyed, the all-important spirit of the law may be broken.

Much modern thinking of medical ethics specifies four principles:

1. Autonomy
   This means the right of a patient to control his own treatment, and the need of the doctor to have the consent of the patient before he starts treatment. (Special rules apply to children or in circumstances where an individual is not able to give consent).

2. **Beneficence**

   The doctor is under an obligation to confer benefits and prevent harm to the patient, and in any action, must weigh up possible good and possible harm to the patient.

3. **Non-maleficence**

   A doctor must not use his power or skill to injure or harm a patient.

4. **Justice**

   Where there are scarce resources of care available to patients, giving care by the best and fairest means.

Doctors in the UK are regulated by and registered with the General Medical Council (GMC). After appropriate professional training, an individual qualifies as a doctor and is entitled to registration. After that, the doctor's conduct is liable to review by the GMC, which will intervene in certain circumstances.

The Professional Conduct Committee of the GMC considers the case of any medical practitioner who is convicted in the British Isles of a criminal offence or who is judged by the Committee to have been guilty of serious professional misconduct. The GMC, through the Professional Conduct Committee, has the power to erase the doctor's name from the register (which means they are no longer a doctor), suspend the registration for up to 12 months or impose conditions for up to three years on the doctor's practise. The Interim Orders Committee of the GMC has power to suspend or impose conditions on a doctor's practise in advance of his care being considered by the Preliminary Proceedings Committee of the Professional Conduct Committee. It will impose conditions where the Interim Orders Committee considers it necessary for the protection of members of the public, or otherwise if it is in the public interest, or in the interests of the doctor, that the doctor's registration be restricted whilst an allegation is resolved. The public interest includes preserving public trust in the profession and maintaining good standards of conduct and performance.

Disciplinary findings within the NHS by a Disciplinary Committee or another body do not amount to a conviction; however, a charge of misconduct may arise out of the facts which have already been considered by such an NHS body.

Many cases referred to the GMC are disposed of at an early stage by a warning letter or a letter of advice (for example, in connection with a minor motoring offence or where a doctor's professional conduct has fallen below the proper standard) without necessitating a full enquiry before the Professional Conduct Committee.

The GMC advises that:

> *"Any abuse of the privileges and opportunities afforded to a doctor or any grave dereliction of professional duty or serious breach of medical ethics may give rise to a charge of serious professional misconduct."*

The key responsibility of a doctor concerns the proper care of a patient. The GMC may institute proceedings when a doctor appears to have failed seriously in their professional duties, for example, by failing to provide necessary treatment for a patient. In general practice, this question is most likely to arise where a doctor has failed to visit a patient or to see a patient who has presented themselves at surgery. These are often matters which are the cause of complaint to disciplinary committees. It is, therefore, essential that General Practitioners have adequate means of ensuring that all requests for visits are properly considered, and that the provisions of Paragraph 17 of the Terms of Service (for Part II GPs) are complied with by practice staff. As noted in Chapter 1, the discipline provisions for Pilot Scheme doctors depend on the Terms of the Pilot Scheme Agreement, but, there is nothing however to prevent a Health Authority or Primary Care Trust (PCT) making a Conduct Complaint to the GMC.

The GMC's guide, *Good Medical Practice*, also provides that, if a doctor has grounds to believe that another doctor or other healthcare professional may be putting patients at risk, the doctor must give an honest explanation of his concerns to an appropriate person from the employing authority, such as the Medical Director, Nursing Director or Chief Executive, or the Director of Public Health, or an officer of the Local Medical Committee and, in doing so, follow any relevant procedures set by the employer. If there are no appropriate local systems, or existing local systems cannot resolve the problem and concern remains, the relevant regulatory body should be informed. Technically, GPs are not "employed" in the terms used in the GMC guidance, but there is no doubt that the guidance applies equally to them.

In discharging their responsibilities to patients, doctors rely on their staff. Obviously, the delegation of certain medical duties is to nursing staff who have been trained to perform specialist functions. A doctor who does delegate must be satisfied that it is proper to delegate this activity, and that the person actually carrying out the treatment or procedure is competent to carry it out. The doctor retains ultimate responsibility for the care of the patient and is responsible if anything goes wrong.

Other areas of concern for the GMC include the improper prescription or supply of controlled drugs. There are clear statutory provisions regulating how such drugs are prescribed and requiring adequate records to be kept. When doctors sign medical certificates, they are under an obligation to take care to ensure that what they are signing is actually true. A doctor who signs a statement which is untrue, misleading or in any way improper, or who breaks the law on drugs, may be liable to disciplinary proceedings.

Other areas of particular concern to the GMC include breach of professional confidence, personal relationships between doctors and patients, improper influence in order to obtain money, abuse of alcohol or drugs, dishonesty, and indecent or violent behaviour.

Professional misconduct

Matters of misconduct considered by the GMC include allegations of improper behaviour which bring the profession into disrepute. This would cover such matters as fraud, violence, drunkenness and inappropriate sexual conduct (especially with patients). The question of sexual relations with patients has long been recognised as professionally problematic. The Hippocratic Oath included this statement:

"In every house where I come I will enter only for the good of my patients, keeping myself far from all intentional ill-doing and all seduction, and especially from the pleasures of love with women or with men, be they free or slaves."

There is considerable research literature (predominantly of American origin) on this ethical problem, and questions of improper sexual advances frequently figure in complaints to the GMC.

Nursing ethics

Like medicine, nursing is a profession which is regulated by members of the profession in the interests of the profession and the public. Nurses have similar codes of ethics and are subject to similar disciplinary proceedings as doctors. The issues faced by nurses and doctors in considering their professional and ethical responsibilities are essentially the same. In the UK, the regulation of nurses is carried out by the United Kingdom Central Council for Nursing, Midwifery and Health Visiting (UKCC).

This statutory body has similar procedures to the GMC, and can suspend or terminate the registration of a member of the profession for misconduct which is defined as:

> *"conduct unworthy as a registered nurse, midwife or health visitor."*

In addition, action may be taken against a professional where it is demonstrated that the fitness to practise of such a practitioner is seriously impaired by illness. In considering issues of misconduct, the UKCC has determined its standard for judgement as follows:

> *"The standard which the Committee takes as its yardstick is not the highest standard which a professional person might obtain, but a standard which can reasonably be expected of an average practitioner."*

The UKCC Code of Professional Conduct for the Nurse, Midwife and Health Visitor is the definitive statement of the general professional obligations of nurses in the UK. Among its key requirements, nurses are obliged to:

- Act always in such a way as to promote and safeguard the well-being and interest of patients/clients.

- Ensure that no action or omission on their part within their sphere of influence is detrimental to the condition of patients/clients.

- Acknowledge any limitations of competence and refuse in such cases to accept delegated functions without first having received instruction in regard to those functions and having been assessed as competent.

- Respect confidential information obtained in the course of professional practice and refrain from disclosing such information without the consent of the patient/client or the person entitled to act on their behalf, except where disclosure is required by law or by the order of the Court, or is necessary in the public interest.

The UKCC emphasises the need for nurses to ensure that they act in a professional way and do not allow their responsibilities as employees to override their professional duty. In considering any case, the UKCC will look at all the facts surrounding it, including the personal circumstances of the nurse concerned and the nurse's overall conduct and behaviour.

Fitness to practise

Doctors

Doctors should have the insight to recognise that, like everyone else, they may become ill and need help. A crucial element of healthcare is the involvement of the sympathetic but dispassionate outsider, who is in a position to consider objectively the needs of the individual. It is for this reason that informed professional opinion is opposed to self-treatment and doctors should, where possible, avoid treating members of their own families. When a doctor seeks treatment from a colleague they are entitled to the same care, concern and confidentiality as any other patient.

On occasion with a "doctor patient", as with any other patient, a question may arise as to competing public interests in maintaining confidentiality and public safety. The National Counselling Service for Sick Doctors is a confidential service provided by the profession.

Use of the service is sometimes initiated by the doctor himself and other times by colleagues concerned that a doctor is not taking appropriate measures to deal with his health problems. Help comes from a doctor from outside the area concerned. Other groups exist to help doctors with health problems; notably the British Doctors and Dentists Group, a support group of recovering medical and dental drug and alcohol users.

Where a doctor is suffering from an infectious disease, that doctor is under a general ethical duty to consider the safety of their patients. The GMC has produced specific guidance, *Serious Communicable Diseases*, with respect to doctors who consider that they may be suffering from diseases such as human immunodeficiency virus (HIV), tuberculosis and hepatitis B and C. The guidance requires such doctors to be tested and, if infected, to have regular medical supervision and seek and adhere to appropriate expert professional advice on any changes or restriction in their practise. Any doctor who is aware that counselling which a doctor has been given with respect to professional activity in this context is not being followed, is under a duty to take steps to warn an appropriate body, such as the GMC. Guidelines have now been introduced with respect to hepatitis B infection and immunisation. Where an individual is E-antigen positive, they are under a clear obligation not to carry out certain procedures. Failure to take advice and modify practise is a criminal offence of committing a public nuisance, and may lead to imprisonment.

A Health Authority has the power to take over the running of a GP's practice. Where a Health Authority is satisfied (after receiving a report from the local medical committee) that, because of a practitioner's physical or mental condition or because of his continued absence, the doctor's obligations under his Terms of Service are not being adequately carried out, it may, with the consent of the Secretary of State, make arrangements for the temporary provision of General

Medical Services (Regulation 25 of a Part II doctor's Terms of Service). There is no comparable provision for Pilot Scheme doctors and if services are not being provided it will be a matter of contract as to the steps to be taken by the commissioner of the services.

The GMC has the power, under its health procedures, to take steps with respect to sick doctors. Section 37 of the Medical Act 1983 provides that, where the fitness to practise of a fully registered person is judged by the Health Committee to be seriously impaired by reason of their physical or mental condition, the Committee may suspend registration for up to a year or impose conditions on it which they consider necessary for the protection of members of the public or in the interests of the doctor.

The Preliminary Proceedings Committee of the GMC can, in appropriate cases, make an interim order suspending or imposing conditions on a doctor's practice in order to protect the public. A doctor has a right to be heard before such decisions, by either Committee, are made. While Health Committee determinations may be appealed on a point of law to the Privy Council, in practice, the findings of the Committee are unlikely to be overturned. Since the powers of the GMC Committees in health cases do not allow it to erase a doctor from the register, some doctors are reviewed by the Health Committee on an annual basis.

Nurses

The Nurses, Midwives and Health Visitors Act 1997 and The Nurses, Midwives and Health Visitors (Professional Conduct) Rules 1993 (as amended by the 2001 Rules) provide for the regulation of the nursing profession and are, in general terms, similar in effect to the Medical Act. A person may be removed from the register if "she has been guilty of misconduct" which includes convictions for criminal offences. Where a nurse has been convicted it is not open to the nurse to try to re-open the question of guilt; however, the fact of a conviction is not in itself determinative of the issue of misconduct. A conviction does not include a sentence of probation or a conditional or unconditional discharge. A nurse may also be removed from the register if:

> *"Her fitness to practise is seriously impaired by reason of her physical or mental condition."*

Unlike with doctors, this is an actual removal from the register rather than simply a suspension. A nurse may apply to be re-admitted to the register when they have been removed, whether for misconduct or ill health.

CHAPTER 3

CONFIDENTIALITY, CONSENT AND PATIENT RECORDS

Confidentiality

Confidentiality forms a central part of the relationship between doctors and patients. It is the patient's right to expect that any information disclosed to the doctor will be held confidentially. The law recognises that there is a public interest in maintaining patient confidentiality and therefore, doctors and their staff are under an obligation to ensure that the rules of confidentiality are followed.

It is very important that staff do not discuss patients where they may be overheard, neither should they leave patient records where others, other than authorised medical staff, may see them. Doctors should try to conduct their consultations with patients in private.

From time to time, a doctor will have to share information about a patient with their staff. It is good practice for doctors to inform their patients that they may need to do this, and, of the reasons for such disclosure.

A doctor should always be careful before disclosing information about their patient and should handle the information so that only those who need to know are informed. The information, which the doctor provides, should be restricted to that which is needed.

The GMC has advised that a doctor who decides to disclose confidential information about an individual must be prepared to explain and justify that decision whatever the circumstances of the disclosure. Doctors who are faced with a difficult decision whether to disclose information without a patient's consent must carefully weigh up the argument for and against disclosure. If in doubt they would be wise to discuss the matter with an experienced colleague or to seek advice from a Medical Defence Society or professional association.

Where information needs to be shared with others working in healthcare, the doctor should ensure that the patient understands what information will be disclosed, however, there will be times when a patient may object. Where a patient objects, the doctor should respect their patient's decision, unless, non-disclosure of personal information could expose others to serious harm. The person, to whom patient information is disclosed, must also be made aware that such information is confidential.

Patient information may be requested for educational or research purposes. Where such a request is made, the doctor has a duty to protect their patient's privacy. The person responsible for maintaining patient information should always ensure that it is protected from improper and unintentional disclosure. The General Medical Council (GMC) provides that, where possible, the doctor should obtain the patient's consent to disclose the information; use anonymous data where unidentifiable data can be used and keep disclosures of this type to a minimum.

In some circumstances, the communication of confidential information may not amount to a breach of confidentiality; for example, where the information is already generally publicly known or where there is a clear public interest that the information shall be disclosed.

Circumstances where disclosure of information is permissible are:

- Where the patient consents

- In compliance with an order of the Court

- In discharge of a statutory duty, for example, to report notifiable diseases etc

- Disclosure to a family or to third parties in the interests of a patient

- Disclosure in the public interest

- Communications with other health professionals for the purposes of treatment, and

- Disclosure for teaching and research purposes.

Consent

To treat a patient without consent may constitute an assault on the patient for which the practitioner may be liable to pay compensation or which may amount to a criminal offence. The more common problem, however, is not that the patient has been treated without consent, but that the patient and doctor have not communicated properly. It is becoming increasingly clear in case law that, in many circumstances, doctors may be held negligent if they have not properly explained the nature of any proposed treatment and the extent of the risks involved. In the context of a claim for compensation as a result of unsatisfactory treatment, consent means more than the doctor obtaining the patient's permission to give treatment. The principle of autonomy is being increasingly enforced in civil courts through cases involving claims that a doctor has been professionally negligent where he has not pointed out to the patient some of the possible risks and problems associated with treatment.

Before a patient undergoes any form of treatment or medical investigation, the doctor must discuss the treatment or investigation with the patient and obtain their consent. There are two types of consent: express and implied.

Express consent is where the patient indicates his or her informed consent in writing or orally. If a patient is capable of providing consent, written consent should be obtained where:

- The treatment or procedure is complex or involves significant risks and/or side effects

- Providing clinical care is not the primary purpose of the investigation or examination

- There may be significant consequences for the patient's employment, social or personal life, or

- The treatment is part of a research programme.

Doctors are required by law, to comply with statutory requirements and although it is certainly desirable to obtain the patient's consent the statutory duty to report (for example, in cases of infectious diseases) overrides any absence of consent.

During consultations, doctors often need to examine patients. Where a patient complies with a procedure, the doctor should be very careful on relying on the patient's compliance as being a form of **implied consent**. Where a patient complies, this does not necessarily mean that the patient has fully understood what the doctor is going to do. The doctor should always ensure that they have provided a clear explanation as to what they propose to do and the reasons why.

When obtaining consent from a patient, doctors have a responsibility to provide patients with sufficient information so that an informed decision can be made. This will involve discussing points such as, the nature of the condition, the treatment required, any risks associated with undergoing treatment and any concerns the patient may have themselves. Any discussion should also involve the doctor providing a balanced view of the options available and explaining the need to obtain informed consent. The main details of any discussion should be noted in the patient's case notes and/or on the consent form.

The GMC stipulates that:

> *"Doctors must work on the presumption that every adult has the capacity to decide whether to consent to, or refuse, proposed medical intervention, unless it can be shown that they cannot understand information presented in clear way."*

A patient is considered to be competent if he or she can understand the information given to them and make a decision on that basis. However, if the GP is uncertain, he should seek legal advice.

Where written consent has been obtained some time before the proposed treatment, it is very important that the doctor or a member of the medical team reviews the patient's decision. The reasons for this are that, the patient's condition may have changed, or there may be new methods or options of treatment which have become available and therefore, the original signed consent form may no longer be effective as sufficient evidence of the patient's informed consent. By reviewing any consent documentation, any further action that may be required, if any, will be brought to light.

There are certain limited situations in which adults may be treated without their consent. The most important of these are, where a patient is so mentally ill or disordered that they are compulsorily admitted to hospital in their own best interest under the provisions of the Mental Health Act 1983 and where the patient is unconscious and needs treatment as an emergency.

There will be situations in which the doctor will be unable to obtain the patient's consent, such as an emergency. In an emergency, doctors may provide medical treatment to patients, however, the treatment should be limited to what is necessary at that time. Treatment will be necessary where it will save the person's life or avoid the patient from deteriorating any further. As soon as reasonably practicable, the patient should be informed as to what was done and why.

Children

For the purposes of medical treatment, a competent child is somebody who can understand the nature, purpose and possible consequences of the proposed investigation or treatment, as well as the consequences of non-treatment.

All young people over the age of 16 can give valid consent to treatment and choose their own doctor without consulting their parents. In practice, many doctors consider it prudent to involve parents in decisions with respect to treatment up to the age of 18. If a person is under the age of 18, then the parent can consent to medical treatment on their behalf.

The respective rights of parents and children have been the subject of much anxious consideration by the courts. It has been held that:

- Parental rights clearly do exist and they do not wholly disappear with the age of majority

- Parental rights exist only so long as they are needed for the protection of the person and property of the child, and

- Parental rights yield to the child's right to make his own decisions when he reaches a sufficient understanding and intelligence to be capable of making up his own mind on the matter requiring decision. In light of this, it has been considered that, the individual child can make a decision, even if the child is under the age of 16.

However, the doctor must always assess whether the child is capable of consenting to or refusing the proposed investigation or treatment. Guidance published by the GMC stipulates that, the following factors should be taken into account:

- At age 16 a young person can be treated as an adult and can be presumed to have capacity to decide

- Under the age of 16 children may have capacity to decide, depending on their ability to understand what is involved

- Where a competent child refuses treatment, a person with parental responsibility or the Court may authorise investigation or treatment which is in the child's best interests.

Circumstances may arise where a child under the age of 16 does not want to involve parents in decision-making concerning health care. This is most likely to arise in the situation where a girl does not wish her parents to know about her contraception. Following the decision in the case of *Gillick v West Norfolk and Wisbech Area Health Authority* [1985] 3 All ER 402 (a case concerning under-age girls receiving contraceptive advice from doctors), it is clear that in some circumstances a doctor can advise, prescribe and treat such a patient without notifying the parents, even though it is illegal for sexual intercourse to occur. When consulted doctors should consider the following points:

- Whether the patient understands the potential risks and benefits of the treatment and the advice given

- The value of parental support must be discussed. Doctors must encourage young people to inform parents of the consultation and should discuss with the patient their reasons for not wishing to do so. It is important for persons under 16 seeking contraceptive advice to be aware that, although the doctor is legally obliged to discuss the value of parental support, the doctor will respect their confidentiality

- The doctor should take into account whether the patient is likely to have sexual intercourse without contraception

- The doctor should assess whether the patient's physical or mental health or both are likely to suffer if the patient does not receive contraceptive advice or supplies, and

- The doctor must consider whether the patient's best interests would require the provision of contraceptive advice or methods or both without parental consent.

Parents are normally considered the natural protectors of children, and a doctor will usually provide care and advice to children in conjunction with, and with the consent of, the parents. There are, however, circumstances where the interests of the parent and the child diverge. The doctor's primary responsibility is to the child and not to the parents. In extreme circumstances (such as child abuse cases) a doctor may be obliged to disclose information about the child without the consent of, or even without notifying, the parent.

Medical records

At the heart of general practice are the medical records of patients. Because General Practitioners take on responsibility for patients indefinitely (unlike hospital doctors who are normally only treating a patient for a specific illness), over time a GP will build up a detailed clinical history of the patient. This will contain information about illness and treatment, and it may also contain more general information about the patient or their family. Under GPs' Terms of Service, they are obliged to keep proper medical records. This will be either on the forms provided by the Health Authority (these forms remain the property of the HA as "computerised records") or in accordance with the provisions of the NHS (General Medical Services) Amendment (No 4) Regulations 2000. "Computerised records" means records created by way of entries on a computer. Similar provisions are set out in the directions relating to the implementation of Pilot Schemes.

The records are held under an obligation of confidentiality to the patient and, over a period of time, many different people will have an interest in them. Where a patient changes doctor, it is important that the doctor forwards the records as soon as possible to the Health Authority for onward transmission to the next GP.

Acts governing access to medical records

The Access to Health Records Act 1990

Although the patient is entitled to protection of the confidential information, until 1 November 1991 patients were not, as of right, entitled to inspect their own medical records. Then, under the provisions of the Access to Health Records Act 1990, patients became entitled to access to their own records. The definition of "record" is wide, and includes both the doctor's notes and may include those of the nurse, health visitor and other professionals involved in the care of that individual. Under the Act, a "child patient" is entitled to access providing the holder of the record (the GP) is satisfied that

> *"the patient is capable of understanding the nature of the application".*

Conversely, a parent shall not be given access unless the GP is satisfied that the child has consented or

> *"is incapable of understanding the nature of the application and the giving of access would be in his best interests".*

The people who can apply for access to the records are the patient, a person with written authority applying on behalf of the patient, a person having parental responsibility for a "child patient", a person appointed by a Court to manage the affairs of an incompetent person and, where the patient has died, the patient's personal representative and any person who may have a claim arising out of the patient's death. Clearly the latter situation may, in some circumstances, create problems and a further provision dealing with the position after the death of the patient states that when an application for access is made after the patient's death, access shall not be granted if the record includes a note, made at the patient's request, that he did not wish access to be given on such an application.

Section 5

Under Section 5 of The Access to Health Records Act 1990 denial of access should take place in the following circumstances:

- No access to a record dated prior to 1 November 1991, except to explain entries after 1 November 1991

- No access to information where the information could cause serious harm to the physical or mental health of the patient or any other individual

- No access which would give information relating to or provided by an individual other than the patient who could be identified from that individual unless the individual concerned has consented or the individual is a health professional involved in the care of the patient

- Except where the application is directly approved by the patient, access shall not be given to any part of the record which in the opinion of the holder of the record would disclose information provided by the patient or obtained as a result of an examination or investigation to which the patient consented in the expectation that the information would not be disclosed, and

- Where the patient has died access shall not be given to any part of the record which, in the opinion of the holder of the record, would disclose information which is not relevant to any claim which may arise out of the patient's death.

Where information is held about an individual on computer, then, under the Data Protection Act 1998 that individual will usually have the right to access to the information. Under the Access to Medical Reports Act 1988, an individual is allowed to access a medical report prepared for employment or insurance purposes. This report must have been prepared on their physical or mental health by a medical practitioner who is or has been responsible for the clinical care of the individual.

The Access to Health Records Act 1990 formerly gave individuals access to manual health records i.e. the sort of non-automated records that the Data Protection Act 1984 did not apply to. However the Access to Health Records Act 1990 has now been repealed by the Data Protection Act 1988 (see below), except for the sections dealing with requests for access to records relating to deceased persons. Requests for access to these records will continue to be made under the 1990 Act.

Requests for access to health records relating to living individuals, whether the records are manual or automated, will now fall within the scope of the Data Protection Act 1988 subject access provisions (discussed below).

The Data Protection Act 1998

The Data Protection Act 1998 gives individuals rights with respect to the collection, use and communication of personal information about them which is held or processed on computer. The individual has rights of access to data about himself, can apply for rectification or erasure of inaccurate data, and is entitled to compensation for distress and harm caused by loss or disclosure of data or harm caused by inaccuracies. The access rights, with respect to health records, are in line with the general access rights considered above. The statute contains eight data protection principles, which guide holders of data and may determine the lawfulness of any particular use of data.

The eight principles are:

1   Personal data shall be processed fairly and lawfully and, in particular, shall not be processed unless one of certain specified conditions are met and in the case of sensitive personal data, at least one of a further set of conditions is also met.

2   Personal data shall be obtained only for one or more specified and lawful purposes, and shall not be further processed in any manner incompatible with that purpose or those purposes.

3   Personal data shall be adequate, relevant and not excessive in relation to the purpose or purposes for which they are processed.

4   Personal data shall be accurate and, where necessary, kept up to date.

5   Personal data processed for any purpose or purposes shall not be kept longer than is necessary for that purpose or those purposes.

6   Personal data shall be processed in accordance with the rights of data subjects under this Act. (The data subject is the individual about whom data is being processed.)

7   Appropriate technical and organisational measures shall be taken against unauthorised or unlawful processing of personal data and against accidental loss or destruction of, or damage to, personal data.

8   Personal data shall not be transferred to a country or territory outside the European Economic Area unless that country or

territory ensures an adequate level of protection for the rights and freedoms of data subjects in relation to the processing of personal data.

The general processing conditions include the requirement that the data subject has given his consent to the processing and that the processing is necessary for the performance of a contract to which the data subject is a party. A further condition which will also be satisfied in the case of GPs is that the processing is necessary for compliance with the legal obligations imposed on the practitioner.

The specific conditions relating to sensitive personal data is that the data subject has given his consent to the processing and that the processing is necessary for medical purposes and is undertaken by a health professional or a person who, in the circumstances, owes a duty of confidentiality which is equivalent to that which would arise if that person were a health professional.

Sensitive personal data means personal data consisting of information as to:

- The racial or ethnic origin of a person.

- Their political opinions.

- Their religious beliefs (or other beliefs of a similar nature).

- Whether they are a member of a trade union.

- Their physical or mental health or condition.

- Their sexual life.

- The commission, or alleged commission, of any offence or any proceedings for any offence committed or alleged to have been committed by him, the disposal of such proceedings or the sentence of any court in such proceedings.

The processing of data is broadly defined and even includes the reading of computer information on a screen.

Medical purposes include the purposes of preventative medicine, medical diagnosis, medical research, the provision of care and treatment and the management of healthcare services.

The person who is the subject of the data is entitled both to know the purposes for which the data is being held, together with the recipients or class of recipients to whom it may be disclosed and the source of the data.

EU Directive 95/46/EC, to which the 1998 Act gives effect, defines the data subject's consent as:

> *"...any freely given specific and informed indication of his wishes by which the data subject signifies his agreement to personal data relating to him being processed"*

There are five points to be noted with regard to consent:

1 "Signify" requires some active communication between the parties.

2 Consent under duress or on basis of misleading information would not be valid.

3 Consent may not be valid for ever and may be withdrawn.

4 Consent must be appropriate in the circumstances.

5 Consent should be absolutely clear, that is: explicit.

The level of consent will vary – in some cases implied consent may be sufficient but in other cases nothing but clear written consent will suffice.

A blanket consent to the processing of personal data is unlikely to be sufficient as a basis upon which to process personal data – particularly sensitive personal data.

In the same way that consent must be "informed", data subjects must be fully aware of the ways in which their personal data may be processed in order for that processing to be considered fair.

Subject to certain exceptions (such as National Security), the data subject, upon making a request in writing and paying the set fee, is entitled, amongst other things:

- To be told by the data controller if they or someone else on their behalf is processing that data, and if so

- To be given a description of:

    a) The personal data

    b) The purpose for which it is being processed, and

    c) Those to whom it is or may be disclosed.

- Further, the data subject has to be told in an intelligible form:

    a) All the information which forms any such personal data

    b) Any information as to the users of those data.

Quality of information held

The accuracy of information recorded on a computer and the effect of recording only "summary" information are important matters.

All practitioners owe a duty of care to their patients and an inaccurate entry, whether made in manual or computer records may, if damage results, give rise to a liability to compensate the patient or his personal representatives. A computer provider will owe a similar duty to any patient and liability could result if it could be established that there was a breach of that duty.

The difficulties which may arise when only "summary" information is available to any doctor accessing the system are major concerns. In ordinary general practice the GP knows the patient and, in almost every case, some of the background information is not written in the record. This is probably acceptable if the records never leave the practice but if computer records are transmitted to another practice or health provider or are used by locum doctors there will need to be a clear note that only "summary" information is contained in the record.

Right of correction

As far as recorded information is concerned, the patient continues to have the same right to have inaccurate information corrected under the 1998 Act as they did under the 1984 Act.

Access fees

Access fees are dealt with by the Data Protection (Subject Access) (Fees and Miscellaneous Provisions) Regulations 2000 SI 2000 No. 191 as amended.

Under these regulations, "Health Records" are defined as any record which consists of information relating to the physical or mental health or condition of an individual, and which has been made by or on behalf of a "Health Professional" in connection with the care of that individual.

A "Health Professional" means any of the following:

- A registered medical practitioner

- A registered dentist

- A registered optician

- A registered pharmaceutical chemist

- A registered nurse, midwife or health visitor

- A registered osteopath

- A registered chiropractor

- Any person who is registered as a member of a profession to which the Professions Supplementary to Medicine Act 1960 extends at present

- A clinical psychologist, child psychotherapist or speech therapist

- A music therapist employed by a health service body, and

- A scientist employed by such a body as head of a department.

It is clear, therefore, that many of the records held by NHS Trusts, surgeries and other healthcare institutions will constitute "Health Records" and therefore fall within the scope of the 1998 Act's subject access provisions.

A maximum fee of £10 may be charged for granting a subject access to health records that are being automatically processed, or that are recorded with the intention that they be so processed.

In effect that this means that a fee of only £10 may be charged for granting access to the sort of records covered under the Data Protection Act 1984.

A maximum fee of £50 may be charged for granting access to manual records (i.e. paper based records), or a mixture of manual records and computerised records where the request for subject access will be granted by supplying a copy of the information in permanent (printed) form.

There is no express provision for any fee to be charged for copying or despatching copies of records. The Data Protection Commissioner advises that the £50 chargeable fee has been set so as to allow for some of the costs incurred to be recovered. The fee was to have been reduced to £10 as from 24 October 2001, but the proposed reduction was withdrawn following BMA pressure.

No fee may be charged where the subject access request is to be complied with other than by supplying a copy of the information in a permanent form i.e. by allowing the applicant to inspect the record.

This provision only relates to requests for access to non-automated records where at least some of the entries were made after the beginning of a period of forty days immediately preceding the date of the request.

This provision broadly replicates the provision of the Access to Health Records Act 1990 that, in effect, allowed patients to look at recently created records without charge.

Medical commentators and organisations have expressed considerable concerns about the provisions of the Data Protection (Subject Access) Regulations but it is not known at present whether the Government will be prepared to make any changes.

It is also the case that these transitional provisions are extremely complicated and specific advice may be needed in cases which do not immediately appear to fall into the above regime. In essence however, it is the case that after October 2001 there will be very few records which will fall under the transitional provisions.

The Data Protection Commissioner is a public officer charged with ensuring adherence to the law and has published codes on various aspects of data protection. The General Practitions Committee of the BMA has issued a code of practice on the Data Protection Act 1998 as it affects GPs. This should be taken into account by GPs in setting their own local procedures for ensuring compliance with the law; the statutory provisions and guidance set out a system of good practice concordant with the ethical obligations of doctors. Most importantly, GPs should ensure that they are properly registered under the Data Protection Act 1998 for all the data they have and for all its uses.

Mental health law

In looking at the law relating to mental health, the issues of correct diagnosis and patients' consent to treatment are brought sharply into focus. As part of the modern reaction to the ethical outrages committed by doctors under the Nazi regime, there has been intense focus on the need for patients' consent before treatment is attempted. From the 1960s onwards it became increasingly clear that in Soviet institutions, some doctors were classifying patients as mentally ill when they displayed patterns of behaviour and systems of belief, which, in liberal democracies, are perceived as proper and praiseworthy.

The law relating to mental health in the UK is an attempt to structure the treatment of mentally ill patients in this highly contentious area, the law aims to provide ethically acceptable responses to the questions of consent and of the diagnosis of illness in order to inspire public confidence, respect the rights of patients and supply clinically meaningful legistlation. The Mental Health Act 1983 was the result of long and detailed consultation and discussion, with the Department of Health struggling to find a structure which was acceptable to all the many interested parties – most notably psychiatrists and groups concerned with the civil liberties of patients. One of the key provisions of the Act, is the right of appeal to the Mental Health Review Tribunal which oversees the use of the compulsory powers contained in the Act. Many thousands of such appeals are made each year.

The Act deals with questions concerning the care and treatment of mentally disordered patients and also deals with problems in the management of their property. In this book we only review those issues relating to compulsory admission to hospital (under Part II of the Act), where GPs are likely to be involved.

The Act defines "mental disorder" as:

> *"Mental illness, arrested or incomplete development of mind, psychopathic disorder or disability of mind"*
>
> (from Section 1(2) of the Mental Health Act 1983)

The Act is careful, in the light of prevailing social values, to restrict the ambit of the definition:

> *"Nothing in subsection (2) above shall be construed as implying that a person may be dealt with under this Act as suffering from mental disorder, or from any form of mental disorder described in this section, by reason only of promiscuity or other immoral conduct, sexual deviancy or dependence on alcohol or drugs."*

Section 2 stipulates that, a patient may be compulsorily admitted and detained for assessment for a period of up to 28 days on the certificate of two medical practitioners stating that the patient is suffering from a mental disorder of a nature, or to a degree, which warrants detention in hospital for assessment, or assessment followed by treatment for a period of time, and the detention is necessary in the interests of the patient's health and safety, or in order to protect others. Admissions under this provision are initiated by the nearest relative or an Approved Social Worker. A patient may be discharged early by the Responsible Medical Officer (RMO), the hospital managers or the nearest relative (the RMO can prohibit a relative-initiated discharge). In addition, Section 4 contains emergency powers for compulsory admission for assessment on the same grounds for up to 72 hours where one doctor (usually the GP) supports an application by the nearest relative or an Approved Social Worker for an admission for assessment, where the delay in obtaining the opinion of a second doctor would cause undesirable delay.

Section 3 provides for compulsory admission for treatment for a period of up to six months, which may be renewed. Here, the application must be supported by a recommendation by two medical practitioners (one "approved" by the Secretary of State as having special experience in the treatment or diagnosis of mental illness). The recommendation must state that:

- The patient is suffering from mental illness, severe mental impairment or psychopathic disorder, or that mental disorder is of a nature or degree which makes it appropriate for them to receive medical treatment in a hospital

- In the case of psychopathic disorder or mental impairment, such treatment is likely to alleviate or prevent a deterioration of their condition, and

- It is necessary for the health and safety of the patient or for the protection of other persons that they should receive such treatment, and it cannot be provided unless they are detained under Section 3 of the Act.

A magistrate has power, on the application of an Approved Social Worker, to grant the police a warrant to enter premises and remove a person believed to be suffering from mental disorder who has been, or is being, ill-treated, neglected or kept under improper control, or is unable to care for themselves if living alone. When the police execute the warrant they need to be accompanied by an Approved Social Worker and a registered medical practitioner.

Caldicott Guardians

Patients have a legal right to privacy. The Caldicott Report (an NHS inquiry into confidentiality) established a number of principles designed to protect the individual rights of patients in respect of privacy. A consultation document was circulated in June 1998 outlining proposals for the introduction of Guardians in the NHS. The Report suggested that there should be Guardians who would agree, monitor and review protocols governing access to patient-identifiable information by staff within their own organisation and also the communication of the same information to and between other organisations. The Guardian's role would be to deal with operational issues concerning aspects of confidentiality, IT and security in relation to patient information.

The principles state that all patients should be consulted before any information about them is used for purposes other than medical treatment. There are no Terms of Service requirements that a GP practice should have a Caldicott Guardian, but an increasing number of practices do so.

CHAPTER 4

MEDICAL NEGLIGENCE

In ordinary Civil Law, compensation can be claimed by one individual against another if they have been injured by that other person's negligence. In order to establish a right to compensation, an individual will need to establish that:

- The other person owed them a duty of care

- They were in breach of that duty, and

- Harm was caused to them by that breach of duty.

Although the rules are themselves easy to state, the working out of those rules against the factual background of contemporary clinical practice can be a matter of considerable complexity.

In medical cases, there is normally no question as to whether or not a duty of care exists. For a General Practitioner, the question normally resolves itself to one of determining whether or not a patient comes within the definitions of a GP's patient contained in either the GP's Terms of Service or as provided for in a Pilot Scheme Agreement. Where a doctor is treating a patient, or is under an obligation to treat the patient (for example, by visiting), then the doctor owes a duty of care to that patient.

The test for the standard of care required of a doctor or of any other person professing some skill or competence, has been set out in the judgement of McNair J in *Bolam v Friern Hospital Management Committee* [1957] 2 All ER 118, where he said:

> *"I myself would prefer to put it this way: a doctor is not guilty of negligence if he has acted in accordance with a practice accepted as proper by a responsible body of medical men skilled in that particular art ... Putting it the other way around a doctor is not negligent if he is acting in accordance with such a practice merely because there is a body of opinion that takes a contrary view."*

This dictum has stood the test of time and, in different words, was repeated by Lord Scarman in *Maynard v West Midlands Regional Health Authority* [1985] 1 All ER 635 when he said:

> *".... I have to say that a judge's 'preference' for one body of distinguished professional opinion to another also professionally distinguished is not sufficient to establish negligence in a practitioner whose actions have received the seal of approval of those whose opinions, truthfully expressed, honestly held, were not preferred. If this was the real reason for the judge's finding, he erred in law even though elsewhere in his judgement he stated the law correctly. For in the realm of diagnosis and treatment negligence is not established by preferring one respectable body of professional opinion to another. Failure to exercise the ordinary skill of a doctor (in the appropriate speciality, if he be a specialist) is necessary."*

In *Bolitho v City and Hackney Health Authority* [1997] 4 All ER 771, the *Bolam* test was carefully considered. It was held that a doctor could be liable for negligence in respect of diagnosis and treatment, despite a body of professional opinion sanctioning his conduct, where it had not been demonstrated to the judge's satisfaction that the body of opinion relied on was reasonable or responsible. In the vast majority of cases, the fact that distinguished experts in the field were of a particular opinion, would demonstrate the reasonableness of that opinion. However, in a rare case, if it could be demonstrated that the professional opinion was not capable of withstanding logical analysis, the judge would be entitled to hold that the body of opinion was not reasonable or responsible. *Bolitho* however is probably of limited application and the *Bolam* test is still the bench mark in the very large number of clinical negligence cases.

It is under The Terms of Service (or their PMS equivalent), that a potential distinction arises between general practice and hospital practice. A patient presenting themselves at a GP's surgery is entitled to a level of clinical competence in the care which the doctor gives them consistent with the knowledge and experience of a skilled GP. The standard of care does not vary according to whether the doctor entered into general practice yesterday or 20 years ago.

Where the practitioner is providing services, such as minor surgery, then the standard of care is that which may be reasonably expected of a GP providing minor surgery. However, if that same GP works as a clinical assistant in a district general hospital performing the same minor surgery, then the duty of care is to be assessed as against the standard that should be expected of an individual holding that post – *Wilsher v Essex Area Health Authority* [1988] 1 All ER 871. In the hospital context, questions could also arise because of differences with respect to the availability of specialist advice or services. In medical indemnity terms, however, in the former case the GP will be responsible for the damage caused, but in the latter, liability may be shared with or wholly attributable to the hospital.

In order to be protected and to demonstrate that the practice which they followed is acceptable to an informed body of medical opinion, it is necessary for a GP to ensure that they are reasonably up-to-date; that is, that they are adopting current practice. Clearly, this is most simply done by reading journals and going on courses. No General Practitioner would be expected to be fully aware of all the potentially relevant clinical developments. However, doctors should ensure that they are constantly learning and (where appropriate) modifying their practice in the light of this new information. Whilst a failure to read one article may not amount to negligence, any General Practitioner who fails, for example, to take the publicly recommended precautions with respect to hepatitis B, will clearly be negligent, even though they might not have been so acting the same way five or ten years earlier. A practitioner may be allowed a reasonable time to come to terms with new developments, but this period of time is limited.

Consequential damage

One of the great areas of difficulty in medical negligence cases, (unlike, for example, motor injury cases), is establishing that, the proven negligence of the doctor caused harm to the patient. In certain cases, it may be demonstrated that the clinical failures had no significant impact on the outcome. In many cases, the condition after treatment is simply the result of the development of the pre-existing condition. The issue of harm has to be demonstrated by the claimant on a balance of probabilities. In *Hotson v East Berkshire Health Authority* [1987] 2 All ER 909, the Court determined that there was a 25% chance that the misdiagnosis had affected the outcome significantly, thus the claimant failed in the action. Where there are many causes of the outcome, the claimant needs to demonstrate that, on balance, the negligence materially contributed to the harm suffered. Another hurdle which claimants may have to surmount is establishing that the loss or injury was foreseeable and not too remote. In *Prendergast v Sam & Dee Ltd* [1989] 1 Med LR 36, CA, it was held that, the GP was liable for the brain damage caused by the pharmacist misreading a prescription.

Burden of proof

In cases of negligence, it is up to the claimant to demonstrate, on the balance of probabilities, every element necessary to establish the defendant's liability. This is so even where a new and innovative or unorthodox treatment is used – Wilsher (supra). In certain circumstances, however, a plaintiff may plead *res ipsa loquitur* – the matter speaks for itself. Its usefulness is in circumstances where the plaintiff is unable to specify exactly what caused the injury. In *Cassidy v Ministry of Health* [1951] 1 All ER 574, Lord Denning stated:

> *"If the plaintiff had to prove that some particular doctor or nurse was negligent, he would not be able to do it. But he was not put to that impossible task. He says, 'I went into the hospital to be cured of two stiff fingers. I have come out with four stiff fingers, and my hand is useless. That should not have happened if due care had been used. Explain it, if you can.' I am quite clearly of the opinion that this raises a prima facie case against the hospital authorities. They have in no way explained how it could happen without negligence. They have busied themselves in saying that this or that member of staff was not negligent. But they have called not a single person to say that the injuries were consistent with due care on the part of all the members of the staff."*

Once the principle is established, the burden falls on the defendant to show that there is a credible alternative explanation which does not involve their negligence. If they are unable to do so, then, liability attaches to them.

Compensation

Where an individual is injured through another's tort, the law provides for financial compensation. The Court endeavours to put the injured individual in the position they would have been in had the injury not occurred. The sums awarded cover aspects of both financial loss (both before trial and reasonably anticipated in the future) and non-pecuniary loss. The latter is compensation to the plaintiff for the pain and suffering and loss of physical amenity (for example, loss of the ability to enjoy a game of golf etc.) which is the result of the injury. In *Wright v British Railways Board* [1983] 2 All ER 698 Lord Diplock stated:

> *"Any figure at which the assessor of damages arrives cannot be other than artificial and, if the aim is that justice meted out to all litigants should be even-handed instead of depending on idiosyncrasies of the assessor, whether jury or judge, the figure must be 'basically a conventional figure derived from experience and from awards in comparable cases.' So Lord Denning MR put it in Ward v James [1965] 1 All ER 563 at 576"*

Since personal injury cases are tried by a judge sitting alone, and there are published guidelines, the compensation for pain and suffering is relatively easy to calculate. The sums involved are surprisingly small when compared with damages awards sometimes made in actions for defamation, where juries assess the damages in a less structured way. The financial loss calculation, where there is any continuing disability, may be complex and involve not merely loss of income, but many related questions such as the need for nursing care. It is possible for the Courts to award provisional damages in circumstances where the course of disease is uncertain, thus enabling the claimant to return to Court in the event of a serious deterioration in their condition.

Where the claimant dies before the case comes to trial, the course of action continues for the benefit of their estate; although clearly the various calculations of loss will be on a different basis.

Common areas of negligence claims

The key areas of responsibility with respect to patients, which are identified in GPs' Terms of Service, are reflected in the pattern of negligence claims against GPs. Some 20-25% of Discipline Committee hearings against GPs relate to a failure to visit. These cases can, in certain circumstances, give rise to claims of negligence where, for example, treatment for meningitis is delayed.

Failures of communication

Many problems can arise through inadequate communication of clinically significant matters between a GP, GP staff, hospital and patient. If the Court considers that the failure is by the GP or their staff, then liability will fall on them.

In *Lobley v Going* (9 December 1985, unreported), a child plaintiff with respiratory difficulties was kept waiting to see a GP for 15 minutes, despite the father having told the receptionist: "He has got worse, he is having a bit of difficulty with his breathing". The Court of Appeal held that, the receptionist had not been clearly told that such circumstances constituted an emergency; accordingly she had not been negligent.

In *Coles v Reading and District Hospital Management Committee* [1963] 107 Sol Jo 115, the claimant, who had crushed his finger, saw his GP after attending at a cottage hospital, where he was told to go to the general hospital. The GP failed to enquire properly of the patient as to what advice he had received and simply changed the dressing. The patient developed tetanus and the court held that the GP was negligent in not making proper inquiries.

In other cases, a failure to take a proper history and a hasty misdiagnosis which could have been avoided if the doctor had listened to the patient, founded successful claims in negligence. Other key areas of difficulty are failure to consider test results and failure to ensure that they are properly acted upon.

Misdiagnosis

Diagnosis is fundamental to the practice of medicine and it is unsurprising that failures of diagnosis, particularly in children, have given rise to a body of claims against GPs.

Referrals should contain sufficient information about the patient's condition and other relevant information to ensure that the hospital is apprised of all relevant factors within the GP's knowledge – including the urgency of the condition.

Prescription

Another significant category relates to the failure to prescribe appropriately, for example, as a result of not establishing the existence of a known sensitivity to a drug. Doctors have been held liable for a pharmacist's incorrectly dispensing when the handwriting was unclear (*Prendergast v Sam & Dee Limited* (supra)). Difficulties can also arise with repeat prescriptions, especially of drugs which may be open to abuse.

Consent

While the issue of consent is considered elsewhere in this volume (Chapter 3), in the context of medical ethics and mental health, it also has direct implications for the lawfulness of medical interventions. In order for consent by a patient to be effective, it must be voluntary, competent and adequately informed. However, these three criteria are not totally independent and they need to be considered in the light of the circumstances of the case. Issues of competency arise with respect to children and those lacking mental capacity; the degree of competence needed will vary according to the gravity of any proposed treatment.

There has been discussion about the extent to which consent is voluntary when it is inadequately informed. If the patient is informed in broad terms of the nature of any procedure and then gives consent, the consent is voluntary. If such consent is not obtained, the treatment may amount to the tort of battery (the intentional application of physical contact to the person without consent or other lawful justification) or the crime of assault. Where such consent has been obtained, a doctor could still be liable in negligence purely for a failure to explain the consequences and hazards of a procedure in accordance with accepted medical practice. In *Sidaway v Bethlem Royal Hospital Governors and others* [1985] 1 All ER 643 it was held that the test of liability in respect of a doctor's duty to warn his patients of risks inherent in treatment recommended by him was the same as the test applicable to diagnosis and treatment, namely that the doctor was required to act in accordance with the practice accepted at the time as proper by a responsible body of medical opinion. Whilst English law did not recognise the doctrine of informed consent, a decision on what risks should be disclosed for the particular patient to make a rational choice whether to undergo the particular treatment recommended by a doctor was primarily a matter of clinical judgement although the disclosure of a particular risk of serious adverse consequences might be so obviously necessary for the patient to make an informed choice that no reasonably prudent doctor would fail to disclose that risk.

In *Sidaway*, Lord Templeman also stated that, when advising the patient about a proposed or recommended treatment, a doctor was under a duty to provide the patient with the information necessary to enable the patient to make a balanced judgement in deciding whether to submit to that treatment, and that included a requirement to warn the patient of any dangers which were special in kind or magnitude or special to that patient. That duty was however subject to the doctor's overriding duty to have regard to the best interests of the patient. Accordingly it was for the doctor to decide what information should be given to the patient and the terms in which that information should be couched. The fact that consent has been obtained should be recorded in the notes, together with a summary of any issues raised by the patient and any information given by the GP.

Product liability

One significant area of development in recent years has been the introduction of the "general safety requirement" with respect to manufactured goods. This covers many products supplied, used or prescribed by GPs, from steroids to sterilisers and sutures. This legislation has its origins in the desire of the European Union to ease trade between member states by ensuring that there is a common basis for liability in respect of defective goods traded in the community. The Product Liability Directive (enacted in the UK as Part I of the Consumer Protection Act 1987) introduces the concept of strict liability on the manufacturer with respect to harm caused by his products. This clearly has great significance for pharmaceutical manufacturers and others supplying materials used in clinical practice.

A product is defective if the safety of the product is not as people are entitled to expect. In determining what it is reasonable to expect, all the circumstances are to be taken into account, including:

- The manner in which, and purposes for which, the product has been marketed, its get up, the use of any mark in relation to the product, any instructions for, or warnings with respect to, doing or refraining from doing anything with, or in relation to, the product

- What might reasonably be expected to be done with, or in relation to, the product, and

- The time when the product was supplied by its producer to another.

For GPs, the key issues therefore are, to ensure that in supplying anything to a patient they are doing so in accordance with the manufacturer's guidelines and that they keep records of the source of materials supplied. In order to ensure that they can identify the supplier in any litigation, doctors should retain supply records for at least 11 years. If a GP is unable to identify the source of defective material (for example, a suture) then they will stand in the shoes of the manufacturer. In any litigation, the claimant will still have to demonstrate that the defective product actually caused the harm complained of. As yet this legislation has not been extensively tested in the courts, but it has caused some concern among manufacturers. Concern has been expressed that, if a single-use product is re-used, then the liability for any defect passes to the doctor. It may also attract criminal liability for supplying a device which does not comply with the Medical Devices Regulations 1994.

Incidence of claims

Over the years, there has been a substantial increase in the incidence of claims of clinical negligence. In May 2001, the National Audit Office found that funds set aside to meet outstanding claims at March 2000 were a staggering £2.6 billion, with another £1.3 billion set aside for incidents not yet reported. However, the incidence of success for claimants in clinical negligence litigation is substantially lower than that for other personal injury claims; the ratio of legal costs to damages recovered is also substantially higher, so that in 65% of settlements below £50,000, the legal and other costs exceeded the damages awarded.

There are relatively few reported cases of claims of medical negligence against GPs. This is clearly for a variety of reasons. However, the following may be of significance:

- The GP tends to have a long-term relationship with the patient; as a family friend they are less likely to receive a complaint

- The complaints procedure to the HA provides a means for patients to raise their concerns

- The system of referral from GP to NHS hospital specialist: moving the focus of care in difficult or acute cases may enable patients to shift the focus of their concern about medical treatment to the hospital

- A patient attending at a doctor's surgery sees a specialist GP providing services. A patient attending at a hospital, while under the care of a consultant, may well be seen and treated primarily by junior doctors in training who are not specialists.

Limitation

The general rule is that proceedings for personal injury must be launched within three years of the cause of action accruing: that is three years after the claimant discovers that they have suffered injury. Although problems can arise where the injury progresses from some minor harm, the rule here is that anything other than trivial harm starts the clock running. In order for time to run, the claimant must know:

- The identity of the defendant

- That the injury is significant, and

- That the harm is attributable in whole or part to the negligent act or omission.

The law allows an extension of time where the claimant is under a disability at the time of the injury, that is under 18 or a person of unsound mind who is incapable of managing their affairs by reason of mental disorder within the Mental Health Act. In such cases, time does not start to run until the individual ceases to be under a disability or dies. If the defendant improperly conceals the facts of the case, this will postpone the running of time until the claimant ought to have discovered this. The Court may disapply the time limits where, in the light of all the circumstances, it is just to do so.

Medical records

In any negligence proceedings, medical records are the crucial evidence. It is therefore essential that they are both adequate and available for use in any subsequent litigation. Given the uncertainties of the limitation period, the length of time they should be retained is clearly problematic. A GP is, under The Terms of Service, or equivalent PMS provisions, obliged to keep records and return them to the Health Authority on the death or de-registration of the patient. However, a GP may also have private patients whose records he will retain. Current guidance from the General Practitioners Committee of the BMA suggests that records for adults should be kept for at least eight years after treatment has been concluded, with a longer period in certain cases, for example, mental disorders and maternity records. It is suggested that records relating to the former, within the meaning of the Mental Health Act 1983, should be kept for 20 years after no further treatment is considered necessary or 10 years after the patient's death if sooner. Records for maternity care and paediatric care should be kept until the child reaches 25 years of age or 26 years if an entry was made when the child was 17 years of age or until 10 years after the patient's death if sooner.

Wrongful life

Lawyers are constantly seeking new ways of helping their clients obtain redress. One recent innovation is the claim for "wrongful life".

These claims are based on the case that the child would not have been born but for an act of clinical negligence. This may take many forms, ranging from a failure to advise properly about the risks of a sterilisation, to the failure of antenatal diagnosis of disability. The extent to which there may be a right to compensation will vary considerably. However, the Court of Appeal has indicated that damages may be awarded for matters such as the mother's pain and suffering of pregnancy and childbirth and the financial costs of bringing up the child.

CHAPTER 5

EMPLOYMENT
LAW

The observations made in this chapter refer only to staff employed by a GP and the relationship between the GP and the employee. It is also of note that, at the time of writing, a new Employment Law Bill is in the process of being published and subsequent changes may affect some of the details in this chapter.

Over the last few years there has been an explosion of legislation in Parliament, which has set out new schemes of rights and responsibilities for employers and employees. There has also been a revised system of courts (the Employment Tribunals) to consider cases and a substantial amount of European Law revising employment rights. This legislation has been the subject of interpretation in many thousands of cases before the Tribunals and Courts. The result is that, a body of law many thousands of pages long has been generated. One effect of all these changes is that the law now recognises that employment gives a status and responsibility to the employee as well as to the employer.

Employers normally require references before they employ a worker. With young workers this is likely to be a school or college reference; after that, it is normal to rely on a reference from the current or previous employer. The employer is not obliged to issue a reference, however, any reference given should be accurate and should state the facts correctly. The previous employer owes the employee a duty to take reasonable care as to the accuracy of the facts contained in the reference.

Employees have the right to a written statement of their terms of employment. The statement should contain the following information:

- The names of the employer and employee

- The date the employment began

- The date on which the employee's continuous employment began (taking into account any relevant previous employment which counts towards this period of employment)

- The scale or rate of remuneration

- Intervals of pay (for example, whether pay is weekly or monthly)

- The terms and conditions relating to hours of work

- Any terms relating to:
    a) Holiday and holiday pay
    b) Sickness and sick pay
    c) Pension and pension schemes

- Job title and job description

- The length of notice required from the employee and the employer to terminate the contract

- Whether the job is permanent and if not, how long it will continue or the date of termination for a fixed-term contract

- The place or places of work and the address of the employer

- Particulars of any collective agreements directly affecting terms and conditions of employment and, where the employer is not a party, the identity of the persons who are parties to the agreement, and

- Disciplinary rules (unless the total number of employees employed by the employer added to the number of employees employed by any associated employer is less than twenty).

If the contract is not going to contain a term relating to one or more of the particulars stated above, this must be stated in the contract. The employee is also entitled to an itemised pay statement, protection from unfair dismissal, rights to redundancy payment and the right not to be discriminated against, on grounds of race or ethnic origin*, sex or marital status, disability or trade union membership. These rights can be enforced by means of an application to the Employment Tribunal.

*[**Note:** Religion is included within ethnic origin.]

The statement must be given to the employee within two months of employment commencing. If some of the details referred to in the statement are contained in full in other documents, the statement can refer the employee to the other documents. This is often the case for provisions, for example, relating to sickness, pension arrangements and disciplinary procedures. Employees are also often referred to documentation relating to health and safety. Where the statement does refer the employee to some other document, the employee must have a reasonable opportunity to read the document.

Provisions relating to the names of the parties, the date on which the employment began, the date on which the period of continuous employment began, the scale or rate of remuneration, pay intervals, hours of work, holidays and holiday pay and the job title and description of the work must, however, be included in one document.

For every employer who employs more than twenty employees, the statement given to employees must include a note specifying any disciplinary rules/grievance procedures which apply to the employment. It is good practice to do this even in the case of employers with fewer than 20 staff.

There are two types of contract most commonly used in employment: the indefinite contract and the fixed-term contract. The indefinite contract terminates when either the employer or the employee gives the required amount of notice. The fixed term contract can be used for both full and part-time work and is used where the employment is to be for a fixed period of time.

Where any of the terms of employment are changed, the employer must give the employee a written statement containing details of the change. This statement must be given to the employee within one month from the date of the change.

Although, a written contract may contain arrangements which allow for changes in matters of pay, place of work and other areas, where a contract is in operation, it is not usually possible to change the contract without the consent of both parties. If the employer tries to change the contract they must do so in a reasonable and fair way. If the employer changes a contract without the consent of the employee, this is a breach of contract. If the change is substantial, the employee may be able to claim compensation for unfair dismissal or redundancy. Clearly, if the change is only a minor one or is to the employee's benefit, it is unlikely that the change will cause any difficulty. Nevertheless, the employer should seek agreement to any change of contract and give adequate notice to the employee of the change. If a dispute does arise, then the Employment Tribunal will need to consider whether the change was a reasonable one in all the circumstances of the business.

Part-time employees

On the 1 July 2000, the Government introduced the Part-time Workers (Prevention of Less Favourable Treatment) Regulations. These Regulations give part-time workers new rights. It is now unlawful for an employer to treat part-time workers less favourably than full-time workers in their terms and conditions of employment in relation to:

- Hourly rate of pay

- Overtime rates

- Contractual sick pay

- Access to occupational pension schemes

- Access to training

- Entitlements to annual leave, maternity, paternity or other leave and career break schemes on a pro rata basis, or

- Redundancy, unless different treatment is justified on objective grounds.

If a part-time employee believes their rights have been infringed, they should write to the employer requesting the employer to provide a written statement explaining the reasons for such treatment. The employer must return the statement within 21 days. If the employee is still unsatisfied that the treatment is not objectively justified, a complaint can be made to an Employment Tribunal.

EU Working Directives

The Working Time Regulations came into force in 1998. They implement the European Working Time Directive. The main effects of these regulations are that they limit the number of hours to be worked per week and to be worked at night by employees and provide certain entitlements to breaks, rest periods and holidays.

The number of hours per week, which an employee can be required to work are 48. However, employees can opt out and work more hours if they wish.

Employees are entitled to:

- A daily rest period of 11 hours in each 24 hour period;

- A rest period of 24 hours in each week;

- A break of 20 minutes if the working day is longer than 6 hours, and

- Four weeks' paid leave per year (up until recently, employees had to be continuously employed for a period of 13 weeks to be entitled to four weeks' leave. However, amendments introduced in October 2001 to the Working Time Regulations extend workers' entitlements to leave). Subject to certain restrictions, all employees are entitled to paid annual leave from the first day of their employment and to compensation for any untaken leave once their contract of employment terminates.

There are a number of exceptions to these regulations which apply to health services. Most of the provisions in collective agreements can be excluded or modified. Certain groups are excluded from the limits on night work, entitlements to breaks, and daily and weekly rests. These include workers involved in services which relate to the care or treatment provided by hospitals.

Discipline and grievance procedures

Employers should have in place their own disciplinary and grievance procedures. The employer should inform their employees as to the steps that can be taken in dealing with matters of discipline or grievance and should clearly indicate the arrangements which should be followed when an employee is dissatisfied with any disciplinary action affecting them.

It is useful for the disciplinary procedures to contain a code of conduct which identifies the type of conduct that would: lead to a warning, would amount to serious misconduct and would lead to a dismissal. The procedures should also state to whom and how employees can appeal against any disciplinary action taken against them.

Further advice and information on good practice and on the ways of dealing with disciplinary/grievance problems can be obtained from the Advisory, Conciliation and Arbitration Service (ACAS).

Dismissal

The most important right given by the statutory framework of employment law is the right, under certain circumstances, to complain to an Employment Tribunal against an unfair dismissal.

In order to present a complaint for unfair dismissal, the employee must satisfy certain conditions. The employee must have at least one year of continuous employment with the employer, however, this minimum period of continuous employment is not required where the employee is dismissed for a reason in connection with pregnancy/maternity leave or health and safety cases. The employee must also be below the normal age of retirement, which means: either the normal retirement age of the business or the age of sixty-five for men and sixty for women (if there is no normal retirement age). In addition, the employee must show that they have been dismissed.

The way in which an employee may be dismissed includes the following:

- Where the employer terminates the contract with or without notice (actual dismissal)

- Where a contract for a fixed term is not renewed, or

- Where the employee terminates the contract in circumstances where they have a right to do so because of the employer's conduct (constructive dismissal).

Once the employee has established that they are eligible, the employer must establish that the principal reason for dismissal falls within one of the following:

- A reason relating to the capability or qualifications of the employee for doing their work

- A reason relating to the conduct of the employee

- That the employee was redundant

- That the employee could no longer continue to work in the position employed without contravening a statutory provision, or

- That there was some other substantial reason justifying dismissal.

Capability and qualifications

In dealing with issues of incompetence the "counselling" of staff and the provision of appropriate training is recognised as good practice. In competence cases, warnings prior to dismissal are usual. This lets employees know that their job is in peril, and helps them to focus on the areas of work and/or conduct that need improvement. Where a warning has been given, sufficient time must be allowed to the employee to bring their work up to standard. Where the issue of capability is concerned with the employee's ill health, an employer must be adequately informed of the medical position. The employer needs to consider how long they can get by without the employee, and whether any alternative arrangements can be made so that the employee can continue in work.

Conduct

Where an employee is dismissed for misconduct, a three-fold test has evolved to assist the Tribunal in determining whether or not the dismissal is fair:

- Did the employer genuinely believe that the employee was guilty of misconduct?

- Was that belief reasonable?

- Did the employer carry out a proper investigation of the matter reasonably?

Redundancy

Redundancy arises either when the employer ceases carrying on the business, or when the employer's requirements for workers has ceased or diminished regardless of whether the amount of work required to be done remains the same. In such circumstances, employees who have been employed for more than two years are entitled to a redundancy payment.

An employer is obliged to consult any recognised trade unions in connection with redundancies. The employer must also consider offering suitable alternative work to any potentially redundant employee, although, the ability of a GP to find alternative work for staff is likely to be restricted. In selecting staff for redundancy, employers are under an obligation not to discriminate on the grounds of sex or marital status, race or ethnic origin, disability or trade union membership.

Where there is a change in the doctors running a Partnership, (and thus a change of employer), the staff will almost certainly be regarded as continuing their employment and therefore, there is no question of redundancy. The position is the same when a single-handed GP retires and another doctor takes on the whole of their practice. Where a retiring GP's list is split between various practices, then a redundancy situation could arise.

Contravening a statutory provision

This covers situations where an employee can no longer work in the position held due to the fact that if they did, it would contravene a statutory provision or a recommendation contained in a relevant provision of a Health and Safety Act 1974 Code of Practice, for example, the suspension from work of a new or expectant mother to avoid risk from any processes or working conditions or physical, biological or chemical agents.

Some other substantial reason

For a dismissal to be justified under this category, it will usually be connected with the employer taking some action to protect their business. For example, the employer may wish to reorganise his business or prevent confidential information from being divulged to a competitor. In these circumstances, the action being taken will normally require the employee to agree to a change in the terms and conditions of their employment. The employer will be required to act reasonably and will need to show that the appropriate procedural steps have been followed.

Once the employer has established a reason for dismissal, it is the Tribunal that decides whether the dismissal was fair or unfair, by considering whether the employer acted reasonably or unreasonably in treating it as a sufficient reason for dismissal. This is the key issue in many hearings, and it is not a matter of whether the Tribunal would have come to the same decision as the employer, but, whether the employer's decision was reasonable, bearing in mind the size and administrative resources of the employer and the choices open to them.

Some of the key points, which have emerged from cases, include the fact that the employer must follow a fair procedure. What a fair procedure is depends upon the circumstances of the case and the size of the employer. In a GP practice, where there is usually only a small group of staff and doctors, it is not usually possible to have a very complicated system for disciplinary hearings.

The Advisory Conciliation and Arbitration Service (ACAS) is a government agency responsible for assisting in the resolution of all sorts of disputes between employers and employees. Among other activities, it has published various codes and handbooks on matters affecting good practice in resolving disputes and handling disciplinary and other questions arising in employment.

Employment Tribunals

An Employment Tribunal consists of three members: a legally qualified chairman and two individuals; one nominated by employers' associations and one by trade unions. The insight and experience of these individuals has been crucial in allowing Employment Tribunals to reflect the realities of life rather than getting too caught up in legal theorising.

Applications to an Employment Tribunal must normally be made within three months of the event complained of (except for redundancy claims). However, in exceptional circumstances the time limit may be waived. Appeals from the Employment Tribunals are made to the Employment Appeal Tribunal, which again consists of a lawyer (in this case a High Court judge or another senior judge) and the nominees of the two sides of industry.

Employees also have the right to settle their claim by going to arbitration through ACAS. The advantage of arbitration is that claims are usually settled more quickly.

If a claim against unfair dismissal succeeds, an employee may be reinstated to their old job with continuous employment or re-engagement, however, Tribunals award this in only a very small number of cases. Where reinstatment is awarded and the employer fails to implement it, then further compensation may be awarded. More usually, where a Tribunal finds that an employee has been unfairly dismissed, the Tribunal makes a financial award consisting of a basic award and a compensatory award. Both of these may be reduced in the light of the conduct of the employee. The basic award is calculated in terms of the length of service and the rate of pay. The compensatory award seeks to compensate the employee for the loss which the employee has suffered as a result of the dismissal.

Discrimination and equal opportunities

The Sex Discrimination Act 1975 (SDA) and the Race Relations Act 1976 (RRA) require employers not to discriminate on the grounds of sex or marital status, or on the grounds of colour, race, nationality, citizenship, or ethnic origin.

These Acts require employers not to discriminate in their recruitment and selection procedures, or in the terms upon which they employ staff, or offer them training, promotion and dismissal, or in any other way treat a person less favourably on the grounds of race or sex than they would treat someone else.

In addition to direct discrimination, indirect discrimination is also prohibited. Indirect discrimination occurs where, while it would appear that treatment is fair, an unjustified condition or restriction effectively means that, in proportion, more people are excluded on the grounds of their sex or race than other individuals.

In selection for recruitment, it is wise to advertise the post and measure the applicants against clear, written and objective standards relevant to the actual performance of the job. An informal method of recruitment, for example word of mouth, leaves the employer open to a charge of discrimination which is harder to disprove. It also deprives the employer of the opportunity of assessing a wide range of possibly very good applicants.

Up until very recently, the burden of proof in certain cases (including a claim for sexual discrimination) was on the claimant. The person bringing the claim had to prove that they had been discriminated against on the grounds of sex. However, Regulations introduced in October 2001, now place the burden of proof on the employer, to show that they did not discriminate against the employee on the grounds of sex. As a result, it appears, there may well be an increase in the number of claims brought and this could affect GPs as well as other employers. It has therefore become even more important to ensure that fair procedures are used and put in place in GP practices.

Another relevant change which is important to note is that, the Commission for Racial Equality is in the process of compiling a code of practice, which would require GPs to keep details of the ethnic origins of their staff.

The particular provisions which apply to the Disability Discrimination Act 1995 require employers not to discriminate against employees who are disabled or have a disability as defined under the Act. The Act does not apply to businesses with less than 15 employees. Full and part-time workers should be included when calculating the exact number of employees.

Maternity rights

Where a woman is dismissed for pregnancy or a reason connected to her pregnancy before the expected date of birth, the dismissal is considered to be automatically unfair, unless, at the date of dismissal, it would be unlawful for the employer to continue to employ her or that the employee was incapable by reason of pregnancy of adequately doing the work for which she was employed. Such circumstances are unlikely to arise in general practice. They are, for example, more likely to affect those working with dangerous chemicals or X-ray equipment. Any reason connected with pregnancy is interpreted very broadly so that an illness associated with, or relating to, pregnancy falls within the definition. There is no qualifying period of employment for bringing a claim in these circumstances.

Under the Employment Relations Act 1999 and the Maternity and Parental Leave etc Regulations 1999, all women, irrespective of their hours of work or length of service, are entitled to eighteen weeks' Ordinary Maternity Leave (OML).

Those employees of who have worked for a continuous period of one year with their employer (by the beginning of the eleventh week before the expected week of childbirth) are entitled to Additional Maternity Leave (AML). AML begins on the day after OML ends and entitles the employee to extend her maternity leave, so that it continues up to the end of the twenty-ninth week after the week of birth.

In order for the OML period to begin, the employee must, at least twenty-one days before she intends to take her maternity leave, notify her employer of:

- Her pregnancy

- The expected week of childbirth, and

- The date on which she intends to start her maternity leave.

The notice is only required to be in writing if the employer requests it.

The employer can also request for the employee to provide a certificate stating the expected week of childbirth, which must, if requested be obtained from a registered medical practitioner or a registered midwife.

Maternity leave cannot be taken earlier than the eleventh week before the expected week of delivery. However, if the OML period has not started by the time childbirth occurs, the OML period is considered to have started on the day the child is born.

If the employee is absent from work during the sixth week before the expected week of childbirth and this is due wholly or partly to pregnancy, her maternity leave will start on that date. If this situation does occur, the employee does not have to inform her employer of the date she intends to take her OML, but must, as soon as reasonably practicable, inform him that she is away from work for a reason in connection with her pregnancy. There is however, no obligation on the employee to inform her employer that she intends to take AML.

During OML, the employee is entitled to benefit from all of her normal terms and conditions of employment, except those relating to remuneration. The employee is entitled to, the right not to be unreasonably refused time off (with pay) during working hours in order to receive antenatal care. The employee should inform their employer of any intended absence relating to this. The employee is entitled to 18 weeks' paid leave and during the first six weeks of OML, is entitled to be paid ninety per cent of her basic salary. The remaining 12 weeks are paid at present at £62.20 per week.

If the employee intends to return to work at the end of her OML period, she does not have to notify her employer of her return to work. She must, however, return to work at the start of the nineteenth week. If she intends to return before the end of the OML period, she must give her employer at least twenty-one days notice of the date on which she wishes to return to work. If this notice is not given, the employer can postpone her return until he receives the appropriate notice, provided that he does not extend the employee's leave beyond the OML period.

During AML, the employee is entitled to benefit from her employer's mutual trust and confidence, to any terms and conditions which relate to the notice provisions of the termination of her contract and disciplinary/greivance procedures and, if a redundancy situation arose, to compensation. With regard to returning to work at the end of the AML period, the rules (as stated above) concerning notice and returning to work after OML apply.

When an employee returns to work after OML, she is entitled to return to the original position she held before she went on her leave and to the same terms and conditions of employment. When an employee returns to work after AML, she is entitled to return to the same job, however, where this is not possible, the employer must offer her another suitable job on no less favourable terms and conditions than her previous position.

Other parental rights

An employee who has completed one year's continuous employment and has or expects to have responsibility for a child, is entitled to take thirteen weeks unpaid parental leave to care for their child at any time up to the child's fifth birthday or until the fifth year of adoption. In order to take such leave, the employee must be a parent of a child (under the age of 5) born on or after 15 December 1999 or must have adopted a child under the age of 18, on or after 15 December 1999.

Both mothers and fathers can take parental leave, and women who do not qualify for AML, may still be able to take such leave if they have one year's qualifying service by the time their OML finishes.

Parental leave can be taken in respect of each child. It must be taken in multiples or blocks of one week and only a maximum of four weeks' leave may be taken in any one year. Upon any request made by the employer, the employee must produce evidence of his entitlement and where possible, the employee must give the employer at least 21 days notice of the date on which they want the leave to begin. However, it is important to note that, there are certain circumstances in which employer may be able to postpone the employee from taking parental leave, provided that (after consultation with the employee), it is rescheduled to a date not exceeding six months after the initial date chosen. If leave is postponed, the employer must notify the employee in writing of the reason for postponement and of the new rescheduled date(s).

CHAPTER 6

HEALTH AND
SAFETY AT WORK

This chapter deals generally with health and safety issues, which are equally applicable to GP premises as to other premises where employees work. There is no specific obligation on Part II GPs to comply with the regulations, although they are required to do so under general law. For PMS contracts, the National Core Contract imposes a duty on GPs to comply with the Control of Substances Hazardous to Health Regulations 1999 (COSHH) and The Health and Safety at Work etc Act 1974 (HSWA) regulations in relation to premises. These regulations are considered below.

General Practitioners employ staff and occupy premises. As such, they have responsibility for much that goes on at those premises. Some of these obligations have evolved over the centuries by the Common Law and require, for example, that GPs are not to be careless. This duty of care and the obligations in the tort of negligence were acknowledged to be inadequate even after the Occupiers Liability Act 1957 was passed. The Act states that, an occupier of premises owed a common duty of care to all their visitors. The common duty of care was defined as:

> *"A duty to take such care as in all the circumstances of the case is reasonable to see that the visitor will be reasonably safe in using the premises for the purpose for which he is invited or permitted by the occupier to be there."*

However, for almost two centuries, Parliament has repeatedly legislated to protect the well being of employees in different industries. This culminated in the passing of the Health and Safety at Work etc Act 1974.

Health and Safety at Work etc Act 1974

The Act provides a general framework for health and safety and is designed to secure the health, safety and welfare of people at work. It also protects others against risks to health and safety arising from working practices and dangerous substances used or produced at work. Under the powers it contains, ministers have produced a large number of statutory instruments on different aspects of health and safety. The whole process has, in recent years, been influenced by the development of European Law in this field.

If an individual is in any way harmed by a breach of regulations made under the Health and Safety at Work etc Act (but not a breach of the Act itself) then they may be able to sue the employer and get compensation for the breach of statutory duty without worrying whether they would be compensated under the law of negligence or contract. Section 2 of the Act makes it the general duty of employers to ensure, so far as is reasonably practicable, the health, safety and welfare at work of all their employee. Section 2 provides that, the duties owed by employers to their employees extend to the following:

- To provide and maintain plant and systems of work which are safe and without risk to health

- To make arrangements to ensure safety and absence of risk to health in connection with the use, handling, storage and transport of articles and substances

- To provide such information, instruction, training and supervision as is necessary to ensure the health and safety of all employees

- To maintain any place of work under their control together with the means of access to the place of work in a safe state without risk to health

- To provide a working environment for staff which is safe without risk to health and adequate as regards facilities and arrangements for welfare at work.

However, it may well be harder for an employer to prove that something is not "reasonably practicable" than it is to prove that they are not being negligent.

Employers also have obligations to ensure that the community at large is not damaged by the way in which they carry on their business. A GP must ensure, as far as is reasonably practicable, that any of their patients using the premises can have safe access to it. This will be particularly important, where many of the GP's visitors are elderly or infirm.

In addition to the duties above, every employer with more than five staff must maintain a written statement of health and safety policy and of the arrangements for carrying out that policy. The policy must be revised whenever necessary and any revisions made must be brought to the attention of all employees.

The aim of the statement is to ensure that safe systems and practices are developed and that staff are involved and understand their responsibilities. Where there is a recognised trade union, it can appoint health and safety representatives. The employer must consult such representatives on all health and safety issues and the representatives must carry out inspections of the premises in order to ensure that there are no hazards to their fellow members of staff.

Duties are not simply imposed on the employer, however. Employees also have obligations, which, while not as numerous as of those of the employer, are important. The proper execution of these obligations is essential if the employer is to comply with the law. Failure by an employee to carry out their health and safety obligations could, in extreme circumstances, lead to prosecution of the employee. While an employee is at work, they have to take reasonable care not only of their own health and safety, but also that of any other person who may be affected by their activities. Where employees are asked to do something by their employer in order to comply with health and safety requirements, the employees have a duty to co-operate so as to ensure compliance with the health and safety responsibilities.

Enforcement

The Health and Safety Commission (HSC) and the Health and Safety Executive (HSE) are two bodies which were set up under the Act. The Act provides that the breach of the duties set out in the Act or under the regulations amounts to a criminal offence. In practice, the enforcement authorities are usually more concerned with ensuring that the law is complied with and that good practice is adopted, however, they will prosecute in serious matters.

Although it is the HSC's duty to promote and further the purposes of the Act, it is the HSE who is responsible, together with the local authorities for enforcing the law. The enforcing authority may appoint inspectors to ensure that statutory requirements are carried out. The inspectors have a number of powers including: the right to enter premises without permission and where they are investigating an incident, for the purposes of that investigation, they can direct that certain areas be left undisturbed. They can also interview and take written statements from anybody whom they believe may have any information which is relevant to their investigation.

Where an inspector believes that a person is contravening or has contravened statutory provisions of health and safety, they may issue an Improvement Notice, which requires the employer to sort things out within a reasonable time. However, if activities carried out involve a serious risk of personal injury, the inspector may issue a Prohibition

Notice to stop those hazardous activities. The employer does, however, have a right to appeal against an Improvement or a Prohibition Notice.

For the purposes of this book, it is not possible to review all the statutory instruments made in connection with health and safety. Some are specific to other areas of activity (for example, harbours and docks), others relate to occupational diseases (such as pneumoconiosis), which are unlikely to arise in employment in general practice. In the Health Service, the Ionising Radiation Regulations and the Asbestos Regulations may well be significant, as X-ray equipment and other radiation sources are widespread and asbestos is used in many older large buildings. However, many regulations are of direct and continuing relevance to general practice and some of these are considered below.

Reporting of Injuries, Diseases and Dangerous Occurrences Regulations 1995

Subject to certain restrictions, where any person dies or suffers serious injuries as a result of an accident in connection with work, there is an obligation to report it immediately to the enforcing authority (usually the local authority). The employer must send a report to the enforcing authority within 10 days on an approved form, unless the employer provides the HSE with a report in some other format which has been approved by it. Where the employee is unable to continue with the work they might reasonably be expected to carry out for more than three days, the employer must make a report to the enforcing authority within 10 days of the accident.

The employer must keep a record of any such reportable event. Details of the incident must be recorded in a record book kept on the premises. The date and time of the incident must be recorded together with the full name of the person affected together with their occupation and the nature of the injury. A brief description of the circumstances of the incident, details of the place where the incident occurred and the way in which the event was reported must also be recorded.

The Control of Substances Hazardous to Health Regulations (COSHH) 1999

These regulations cover any form of substance, whether gases, liquids or solids, and any type of material, including bacteria and viruses, that are capable of damaging health through being absorbed, injected, inhaled or ingested and which may be encountered at the workplace. The employer is under a duty to ensure that exposure of individuals to the hazardous substance is prevented or, if this is not reasonably practicable, adequately controlled. An employer cannot carry out any work, which involves exposure unless:

"he has made a suitable and sufficient assessment of the risks created by that work to the health of those employees and of the steps that need to be taken to meet the requirements of these regulations."

This assessment must be reviewed on a regular basis and where changes in the assessment are needed, those changes must be made. In addition, the employer must carry out health surveillance, exposure monitoring and the use of control measures. Most importantly, an employer who exposes any of their employees to these substances is obliged to provide that employee with suitable and sufficient information, instructions and training to know the risks to health created by such exposure and the precautions that should be taken. The employer should also provide employees with personal protective equipment and should ensure that such equipment is properly used or applied.

In general practice, one of the key issues is the exposure of individuals to blood-borne pathogens. Following of an appropriate code of practice, such as the British Medical Association's code on the use and disposal of sharps, should help to ensure protection of staff. In addition to the health and safety legislation, there are strict regulations covering the handling and disposal of clinical waste, such as bloodstained bandages and other material which may create a hazard. As well as the infection hazard, a GP's surgery may contain various chemicals which need to be handled and stored in accordance with COSHH.

The following regulations place a requirement on employers to assess risks to health and safety and to take measures to reduce any risks and employees are under a duty to co-operate and assist employers in implementing these regulations.

The Management of Health and Safety at Work Regulations 1999

These regulations require employers to conduct and report assessments of risks to the health and safety at work of their employees and others. In order to comply with the duties imposed by the statutory provisions, employers are required to take all practicable steps to eliminate the identified risks and to set up procedures for dealing with the serious risks.

Regulation 3 requires employers to carry out a "risk assessment". Employers are required to:

"Make a suitable and sufficient assessment of the risks to the health and safety of his employees to which they are exposed whilst they are at work and the risks to the health and safety of persons not in his employment arising out of or in connection with the conduct by him or his undertaking for the purpose of identifying the measures he needs to take to comply with the requirements and prohibitions imposed upon him by or under the relevant statutory provisions."

The process followed for a risk assessment should be practical and should involve both employees and safety representatives. The Approved Codes of Practice made under the Health and Safety at Work Act 1974 set out a number of general principles which the risk assessment should achieve.

In general practice surgeries, there may be many hazards associated with the equipment used and the procedures carried out. Employers must train staff and supply relevant health and safety information to their employees. The risk assessment is fundamental in all health and safety work.

The Personal Protective Equipment at Work Regulations 1992

These require employers to provide employees with personal protective equipment appropriate to health and safety risks in their work, except where other measures to eliminate these risks have been implemented. In a GP's surgery, an obvious example of this would be ensuring that all members of staff who need them, have access to protective gloves.

The Provision and Use of Work Equipment Regulations 1998

These regulations require employers to assess the risk to health and safety caused by work equipment, including the risk generated by cleaning and maintaining the equipment. Employers must ensure that work equipment is maintained in a good state of repair. Employees who use work equipment must be provided with health and safety training and information about the use of the equipment. In general practice, one common source of hazard is poorly adjusted and maintained autoclaves and sterilisers. Under these regulations, GPs have to ensure that the equipment is, and continues to be, safe and is used in a safe way.

The Health and Safety (Display Screen Equipment) Regulations 1992

These deal with the working arrangements for computers and word processors. They require employers to modify workstations, work equipment and working practices to eliminate risks to health and safety of employees using display screen equipment.

In order to comply with the measures under these regulations, the employer is under a duty to provide adequate health and safety training to employees who may be required to use any workstation and to provide information about all aspects of health and safety in relation to the employees' workstations. There is a requirement to ensure that employees are provided with appropriate eyesight tests. The employer is also required to:

> *"so plan the activities of users at work in his undertaking that their daily work on display screen equipment is periodically interrupted by such breaks or changes of activity as to reduce their workload at that equipment."*

The Manual Handling Operations Regulations 1992

These regulations require employers to assess the health and safety risk to their employees at work while lifting, handling and carrying and to take all practicable steps to eliminate the identified risks. Where staff may need to assist patients, proper training in lifting will be necessary.

The Workplace (Health, Safety and Welfare) Regulations 1992

These regulations require employers to assess the risk to the health and safety of their employees in the workplace. They lay down minimum requirements with respect to equipment, ventilation, temperature, lighting, cleanliness, workspace, windows, traffic routes, sanitary conditions, eating facilities and changing areas.

NHS zero tolerance to violence campaign

The issue of violent behaviour and the level of threat from some patients in general practice has become a growing concern for the profession. The Department of Health (DOH) recognises that action must be taken in order to create a safer environment for those who work in general practice. In October 1999, the DOH launched the NHS zero tolerance campaign. The aim of the campaign is to stop violence against staff working in the NHS and to highlight to the public and to all staff, that the NHS is dealing with the issues of violence.

Violence in general practice is defined as:

> *"Any incident where a GP or his/her staff are abused, threatened or assaulted in circumstances related to their work, involving an explicit or implicit challenge to their safety, well-being or health."*

The DOH recognises that, as the number of violent incidents vary according to each individual Health Authority, a national solution to the problem is unlikely to work and that therefore, it is important to have mechanisms in place in order to record and monitor violence against staff on a regional basis. The DOH has published a number of Health Service Circulars, which set out local action that can be taken by the NHS Trusts, Health Authorities and Primary Care Trusts (PCTs), and how GPs can become more involved in local initiatives to deal with violence. Further information on this issue can be obtained from the Department of Health's website – www.doh.gov.uk.

There are a variety of steps which may be taken to discourage violence; these include training employees, changing the layout of waiting areas and providing more information to patients. The policy for dealing with violence should be included in the health and safety policy statement so that all employees are aware of it, can co-operate with it and can correctly report any incidents.

Employment and health and safety

Health and safety is a key issue in employment. On occasions, disputes about health and safety will cause problems between the employer and employees. Employment law also provides some protection to employees who have been dismissed because they carried out proper health and safety activities or, in circumstances of danger which the employee reasonably believed to be serious and imminent, took or proposed to take appropriate steps to protect themselves or other persons from that danger.

It is clearly in the interest of both employer and employees that there is real understanding of health and safety issues in the work force, and that problems can be addressed in a spirit of co-operation rather than confrontation.

CHAPTER 7

DOCTORS AND
THE COURTS

The Courts

Dealing with Courts and lawyers is a normal, but usually unwelcome, part of clinical practice. Although many regret the fact, the gravity and importance of medical work makes it almost inevitable that doctors will be involved in matters where they may eventually be required to give evidence. Furthermore, from time to time GPs will be under a professional obligation to report matters to public authorities which may well involve subsequently giving evidence. Courts vary in their procedures and discharge many different functions.

The procedure in a Coroner's Court is inquisitorial: that is, the coroner decides who should be called and asks most of the questions. A coroner may sit without a jury save in the following cases specified by statute where there is reason to suspect:

1   That the death occurred in prison or in such place or in such circumstances as to require an inquest under any other Act

2   That the death occurred while the deceased was in police custody or resulted from an injury caused by a police officer in the purported execution of their duty

3   That the death was caused by an accident, poisoning or disease notice of which is required to be given under any Act to any government department, to any inspector or other officer of a government department or an inspector appointed under the Health and Safety at Work etc Act 1974, or

4   That the death occurred in circumstances the continuance or possible recurrence of which is prejudicial to the health and safety of the public or any section of the public.

In other Courts, the procedure is adversarial: that is, the claimant and/or prosecution and defendant attempt to establish one view of the facts or to cast doubt on another. With regards to the Civil Courts, the Civil Procedure Rules 1998 led to a fundamental reform of the ethos and procedure of civil justice under which the previous ability of the parties to control the pace and the direction of the proceedings is now constrained. In Civil Courts, except for a very few matters, the jury has been abolished. A criminal case may be tried by:

- A single professional magistrate

- A bench of lay magistrates

- A judge sitting with a jury in the Crown Court (on not guilty pleas) and with magistrates when dealing with appeals from a Magistrates' Court, or

- By judges in the Court of Appeal and the House of Lords.

The doctor as a witness

A GP may be before the Court as a party to proceedings or as a witness. In this section the focus is on the doctor as a witness. (The following section deals with the GP's accountability to the courts and the GMC.)

There are, in essence, three kinds of witness, an ordinary witness, a professional witness and an expert witness.

An ordinary witness is a witness as to fact: for example, a GP who sees a crime being committed might be asked to give evidence. More frequently, GPs will be called to give evidence with respect to patients whom they have treated following an assault. Here, they might give evidence of identification, the injuries observed and the treatment given and, although the GP is a witness, the evidence they give arises out of their clinical work and they are known as a professional witness.

In clinical negligence cases there will usually be medical expert witnesses for all parties but where it is possible for the question of expert evidence to be dealt with by a single expert the Court normally directs that the parties should agree the appointment of the expert between themselves. If this is not successful the Court may make an appointment from a list agreed between the parties or, otherwise, request the appropriate experts' professional body to appoint the expert. The instructing parties are jointly and severally liable for payment of a joint expert's fees unless the Court has directed otherwise.

It is preferable for doctors to ensure that they have close liaison with the solicitor for the party for whom they are giving evidence so that they are kept fully informed of progress and consulted with respect to availability for hearing dates. Notice of listing of cases in the County Court, where damage claims of less than £50,000 are heard, and in the High Court should be served on the parties at least three weeks before the hearing unless they agree otherwise or the Court orders shorter service. It is extremely important that, as soon as possible, an expert witness gives a list of the dates on which they will be unavailable to attend the trial, together with reasons to the solicitor by whom they have been appointed, to assist the solicitor to avoid the trial being listed on those dates when the expert witness is unavailable.

If a solicitor is concerned that a witness may not attend Court then they may ask the Court to issue a witness summons. This is an order of the Court requiring the witness to attend Court on a specific date or dates and failure to comply with the order amounts to contempt of Court. In some circumstances the Court may set aside a witness summons: for example, in one case a party wished to call a certain expert but was unable to afford her fee; the expert was unwilling to give evidence without a fee.

Where GPs are asked to prepare reports, it is important that they know what information is required in order to avoid irrelevant comment. The report must include the following points and must:

1   Be addressed to the Court

2   Give details of the GP's qualifications and relevant material upon which they have relied

3   Give details of the patient, their general health and as much history as is necessary stating what examinations and/or tests were carried out with the relevant dates and whether any witnesses were present

4   Include, in summary, any range of opinions and give reasons for the opinion they have reached

5   State that the doctor has understood and discharged his duties to the Court

6   Contain a statement summarising the facts and instructions, both written and oral, given to them which are material to the opinions expressed in the report or upon which those opinions are based, and

7   Include a signed statement of truth, for example 'I believe that the facts I have stated in this report are true and that the opinions I have expressed are correct'.

An expert can make a written request to the Court for any direction that will assist him in carrying out his task.

The Court will not permit oral expert evidence unless the Court considers it to be necessary in order to secure a just outcome to the dispute and, where each party has appointed its own expert with the permission of the Court, the Court will usually direct that the experts discuss the case to try and narrow down the issues and, if possible, reach agreement. If it is convenient and cost efficient, experts will meet face-to-face but the Court may give directions that the experts should communicate either by telephone or by a video conference. After their discussions the experts are normally requested to prepare a statement for the Court setting out the issues on which they agree or disagree with a summary of their reasons for any disagreement. The statement may be used as a basis for any party upon which to cross-examine an opponent's expert witness.

Any agreements reached between experts following discussions will not be binding on any parties unless they expressly decide to accept them. If an expert changes his opinion as a result of the discussion, the party by whom he is being instructed will have to decide whether or not to accept the expert's new position. Whatever decision is taken the expert is immune from being sued in these circumstances. This is because such immunity is justified, as a result of public interest, in facilitating full and frank discussion between experts before trial. Consequently, an expert should be free to make proper concessions including those which depart from advice previously given to the party who retained him.

It is not for a party or any legal representative to specify what an expert puts in his report. In *Whitehouse v Jordan* [1981] 1 All ER 267 Lord Wilberforce said:

> *"While some degree of consultation between experts and legal advisers is entirely proper, it is necessary that expert evidence presented to the Court should be, and should be seen to be, the independent product of the expert, uninfluenced as to form or content by the exigencies of litigation."*

Where a case settles out of Court doctors must make the care of the patient their first concern. If in the course of the case the doctor learns of information that indicates that unless further actions are taken the patient will continue to be at risk, then they are obliged to act on the information. Signing a contract to remain silent will, in any case which has settled out of Court and where patients may continue to be at risk, put a doctor in the position of being forced to satisfy their professional ethical obligations and break the contract.

Doctors often complain about the delay in resolving questions of fees in cases in which they are involved. The level of fee which may be payable depends on the nature of the witness. If a doctor is there as a professional witness: that is, a witness as to fact dealing with a matter which arose in their professional practice, then the Lord Chancellor's Department and Legal Aid recognise this and a higher rate of fees may be awarded than are normally paid to witnesses. Where a doctor is an expert witness and thus a volunteer, the doctor sets the level of the fees and agrees this with the solicitor for the party which has requested the doctor to act as an expert.

In civil proceedings, doctors should try to arrange that their fees are agreed in advance and paid as the work proceeds. Where a solicitor is acting under the Legal Aid scheme, this is still possible as the solicitor can seek prior approval from the Legal Services Commission. In non-Legal Aid cases, the solicitor should pay the bills as they are presented. Where there is a dispute over the payment of fees, a doctor can seek the intervention of the Solicitors' Complaints Bureau; however, if there is only an agreement to pay "reasonable costs", then the Bureau is unable to assist, and in default of agreement the only recourse is to the Courts. As a general principle, unless there is agreement to the contrary, a solicitor is personally responsible for paying the proper costs of any professional agent or other person whom he instructs on behalf of his client, whether or not he receives payment by his client.

If possible, doctors should negotiate with solicitors a provision that if a Court hearing is cancelled at short notice (for example, 48 hours) a proportion of the fee for the hearing should be payable. This should compensate for the expense of re-arranging commitments and hiring a locum.

In criminal cases, it is normally necessary to wait for the conclusion of the case for payment for preparation work. The attendance expenses and fee are claimed from the Court and are subject to guidance issued by the Lord Chancellor.

Requests for the disclosure of medical records for the purpose of litigation

Where doctors receive requests from patients for information or the release of their medical records for the purposes of litigation they should first determine whether the patient concerned, possessing capacity to do so, has given express consent to that release of information. If the GP is satisfied as to consent, then consideration should be given to the Access to Health Records Act 1990 and the Data Protection Act 1998 (considered in Chapter 3). However, as a general approach, a doctor will wish to comply with a patient's request for the release of records for the purpose of litigation since to do so is to act in accordance with the patient's interests.

Where there is any question of proceedings for clinical negligence, GPs should obviously consult their Medical Defence Organisation as soon as possible.

The Courts, some tribunals and persons appointed to hold enquiries have legal powers to require that information be disclosed which may be relevant to matters within their jurisdiction. The High Court and the County Court have the right to order disclosure of medical records under Section 33 of the Supreme Court Act 1981 and Section 52 of the County Court Act 1984 before any proceedings are issued if they consider it appropriate to allow the applicant to find out without undue delay whether or not they have a case. The Court may make the order for disclosure of medical records under Section 34 of the Supreme Court Act 1981 and Section 53 of the County Court Act 1984 after proceedings have been issued. In the case of confidential documents which are not privileged the Court may impose terms limiting who may inspect them: for example, a potential or actual litigant, their legal advisor and any professional adviser nominated by the Court. Where there is a personal injury, action problems are sometimes experienced in respect of the extent of disclosure of the claimant's medical records however, the general rule is that all the records should be disclosed to the extent necessary for a fair outcome to take place.

In criminal cases a witness summons to produce medical records should be issued only where it is shown that there are substantial grounds for believing that the records contain relevant matters. The person seeking the witness summons must state specifically what information they require, why they believe that the third party has access to the information and why it is relevant. They must also persuade the Court that the witness will not produce the documentation voluntarily: for example, when a doctor has refused to release medical records because the patient has not consented. If medical records are requested a doctor has seven days to notify the Court if they wish to make written or oral representations. Again, however, if a witness summons is issued the records must be released to whoever the Court directs.

The Coroner's Court is a Common Law Court of Record and a Court of Special Criminal Jurisdiction and the Court's function is to inquire into the death of any person whose dead body is lying within the Coroner's jurisdiction, if there is reasonable cause to suspect that such person has died a violent death, or an unnatural death, or a sudden death of which the cause is unknown, or if the person has died in prison, or in such place or under such circumstances as to require an inquest in pursuance of any Act of Parliament.

It is accepted practice for GPs to report to the Coroner any cases of doubt or suspicion. These include:

- Where an accident in any way contributed to the cause of death, for example, where septicaemia has set in

- Death related to chronic or acute alcoholism, poisoning, or drug or substance abuse

- Death where drug therapy, anaesthesia or a surgical procedure may have contributed to death

- Stillbirths where there was a possibility of the child being born alive

- Death where the deceased suffered from an industrial disease

- Death where the deceased was in receipt of a disability or war pension

- Death of a foster child

- Death where ill-treatment or neglect hastened death.

The Coroners' Courts have the right to require the disclosure of health information. Health service bodies are not required to obtain consent in order to comply with any direction to supply data to a Coroner's Court although they should notify the responsible health practitioner and the person concerned if possible.

Coroners are empowered to call doctors to give evidence and to order post-mortems. Specifically, the Coroner may summon as a witness any legally qualified medical practitioner appearing to them to have attended at the death of the deceased or during the last illness of the deceased or, where it appears to them that no such practitioner so attended the deceased, any legally qualified medical practitioner in actual practice in or near the place there the death occurred. Any medical witness so summoned may be asked to give evidence of how, in their opinion, the deceased came to their death. A doctor is liable to a fine if he fails to obey the summons of a Coroner without good and sufficient cause. Again, where there is any question of medical misadventure or negligence, doctors should contact their Medical Defence Organisation.

The general ethical obligation of confidentiality is discussed elsewhere (see Chapter 3), however, when a patient has not given consent for the disclosure of medical records, doctors are nonetheless justified in disclosing information when they believe (on reasonable grounds) that a Court or tribunal (with the recognised power to do so) has authorised it. In such cases, the doctor must disclose the records to whom the disclosure has been directed and exactly in accordance with the order that has been made.

If a conflict arises because a Court order requires disclosure of sensitive health information provided in confidence which may reveal personal health information which the doctor considers is not relevant to the case, or when disclosure of the record may also reveal personal health information about a third party, a doctor should then make their ethical objections known to the judge or the presiding officer. Having done so, and if the judge or presiding officer insist upon the release of the information, the doctor who does not comply will then be in contempt of Court. Where disclosure of medical records is ordered by a Court, the doctor should inform the patient at the earliest possible opportunity.

Accountability to the Courts and the GMC

A doctor who negligently causes injury to a patient (whether NHS or private) may be sued by that patient for the harm caused. These proceedings will be heard in the High Court or County Court, and the GP will usually be represented by their Medical Defence Organisation or Medical Indemnity Insurer. In certain very extreme cases, where it is alleged that a doctor did not have the consent of the patient (see Chapter 3) to an operation or where the treatment was so reckless that it caused death, a doctor may face criminal charges arising out of their practice.

A GP must not allow his views about a patient's lifestyle, culture, beliefs, race, colour, gender, sexuality, age, social status or perceived economic worth to prejudice the treatment they provide or arrange (General Medical Council: "Good Medical Practice"). Discrimination is also an important issue in employment law (Chapter 5).

All doctors practising in the UK are obliged by law to be registered with the General Medical Council. The basic role of the GMC is the maintenance of registers of medical practitioners who are fit to practise. The GMC does this by supervising the education of doctors, registering them, advising them by the publication of guidances, and by erasing, suspending or imposing conditions on their registration in the event of serious ill-health or misconduct (Chapter 4).

Conclusion

Doctors should help the Courts by being clear about their role as doctors, and should work with lawyers to ensure that the doctor's time, the lawyer's time and the Court's time is used effectively. This way doctors are best able to discharge their obligations to their patients, and also their obligation to society at large by assisting in the fair and effective administration of justice.

CHAPTER 8

THE MEDIA AND DEFAMATION

The media

As each year passes there is an increase of media interest in the medical profession, especially in relation to the work of GPs. Doctors are important figures in their local communities and will sometimes be called upon by the press and local broadcasters for comments on medical issues, which are of public concern. This is especially true of doctors who are members of a Local Medical Committee (LMC) or who hold other offices and are seen as spokesmen for the profession. Obviously, good publicity is of substantial benefit to the profession. There is, consequently, a substantial opportunity to gain public approval, inform public debate and educate the public, both in personal health matters and in questions of local and national health policy through the media.

Comments to and interviews with the media

If a doctor is approached for comments or to give an interview, then, providing it is professionally appropriate to do so, the doctor should consider the request carefully and their deliberations should include the matters set out in the following paragraphs.

Where comments requested by the media, or the subject of interviews, would include information about individual patients, doctors must respect patients' right to privacy. Before releasing any information, it is necessary for a doctor to bear in mind that information which they have learnt in a professional capacity should be regarded as confidential, whether or not it is in the public domain, and that doctors should always behave in accordance with the best medical interests of the patients. As patients can be identified from information other than their names and addresses, doctors must obtain explicit consent from patients before discussing matters with journalists that relate to the care of particular patients. It is also very important for a doctor to remember that their remarks are attributable only to themselves (as opposed to an association, authority or professional body) unless they have been otherwise authorised.

In respect of the written media, enquiries should be made of the journalist to establish the exact parameters of the questions they are asking. It is also useful for the doctor to write down notes of what they wish to say.

Before agreeing to an interview a doctor should establish:

- The context and content of the programme, publication or article – what is to be discussed, who is to be the interviewer, are they likely to be friendly or hostile and who else is to appear on the programme

- The logistics – when and where the interview will take place, whether it will be live or recorded, and how long it will take.

If doctors agree to be interviewed, they should prepare carefully the key points that they wish to put over. It is obviously preferable, although sometimes difficult, to be positive and straightforward, and to avoid being distracted into side issues or talking too much. Above all, a doctor should bear in mind the audience they are trying to reach and the likely impact of the interview on them.

GMC guidance on advertising a doctor's services should also be taken into account in contacts with the media. Where a doctor is appearing as a spokesman for the BMA, the GPC or an LMC, no problems regarding advertising issues should arise. Care should be taken however, to ensure that where a doctor is broadcasting or writing on clinical issues, no implication arises that there is a recommendation to consult that particular doctor. Where a doctor appears regularly advising on medical matters, it should be explicitly stated that the doctor cannot offer individual advice or see individual patients as a result.

The position is different, and potentially more difficult, where a doctor is professionally involved in a news story. This can happen in a variety of ways, but commonly arises when an individual patient is unable to obtain treatment which they (and perhaps the GP) think appropriate. Here, where the patient has consented to a discussion of the need for medical treatment, the GP may be cast in the dual roles of advocate on behalf of the patient and of explaining the context of the difficulty in terms of the availability of resources and other issues. In other cases, particularly those involving children, actual or potential Court proceedings (where issues of contempt of Court arise) or where the conduct or competence of a doctor is in question, it will rarely be appropriate to make any public statement and advice should always be sought beforehand.

Defamation

In any communication an individual makes to one person, which deals with the affairs of another, there is a danger, however remote, that the communication will be defamatory. This area of law is extremely complex; so much so, that there is not a single clear definition of what defamation is, although some accepted definitions include:

> • *"A statement concerning any person which exposes him to hatred, ridicule or contempt or which causes him to be shunned or avoided or which has a tendency to injure him in his office, profession or trade." – Parke J in Paramiter v Coupland [1840] 6 M&W 105*

- *"A false statement about a man to his discredit." – Cave J in Scott v Sampson [1882] 8 QBD, 491*

- *"Words which tend to lower the person in the estimation of right thinking members of society." – Lord Aitkin in Sim v Stretch [1936] 2 All ER, 1237*

In broad terms, libel is the written or broadcast word and includes not only printing or writing but also films, video tapes, cassettes, faxes, electronic mail and the internet. Radio and television broadcasts and theatre performances are all "permanent forms of libel" which is defamation in a permanent and visible form. Slander, is defamation by spoken words and by disparaging gestures or actions and is actionable only if the claimant can establish that they have suffered an actual loss, usually of some measurable financial benefit, except where:

1   The words impute a crime for which the claimant could be imprisoned

2   The words are calculated to disparage the claimant in any office, trade, business or profession or calling held at the time

3   The words impute to the claimant a contagious or infectious disease, or

4   Where the words impute adultery or unchastity to a woman or girl (Slander of Women Act 1891).

A claimant in defamation proceedings has to show that the words complained of were defamatory, referred to them and were published: that is, communicated to a third party by the defendant. If they succeed in doing so, the defendant must then establish a defence in order to escape liability.

The substantive defences to a claim of defamation for which the onus of proof is on the defendant are as follow:

Justification

"Justification" can be described as proving that the words were true. A statement is justified if it is true in substance and in fact. However, the burden of proving the truth of a statement falls upon the individual who asserts that truth, and this may not be easy to do where the "truth" is only known through rumour. Proof of the defendant's belief in the truth of the words is not sufficient. This defence applies to statements of fact, as distinct from comment or expressions of opinion. To succeed, the defendant must prove the truth of the gist or sting of the libel.

Fair comment

"Fair comment" can be described as making a statement on a matter of public interest in good faith and without malice. Fair comment protects the honest expression of opinion, however unreasonable. The facts on which the comment is based must be true and be proved by the defendant to be true at the time the comment is made. If the defendant is not able to prove the truth of all the facts, the defence of fair comment can still succeed if the comment can be shown to be fair in relation to the facts which can be proved to be true.

Privilege

"Privilege" can be described as the plea that the words were published on an occasion of absolute or qualified privilege. Privilege applies to certain circumstances where false statements about another person do not give rise to liability.

Absolute privilege

The occasion of absolute privilege may be clarified as:

- The administration of justice

- Reports of Court proceedings

- Parliamentary proceedings and papers

- Affairs of state, and

- Other express statutory instances.

If a witness in a case chooses to use the opportunity of absolute privilege to deliberately defame a third party, that third party will have no recourse to defamation unless the statement is repeated outside the protection of the Courts.

Qualified privilege

Qualified privilege relates to statements which are fair and warranted by any reasonable occasion or exigency, and which are honestly made. Such communications are protected for the common convenience and welfare of society; and the law has not restricted the right to make them within any narrow limits. The defence of qualified privilege is however defeated if the claimant can show that the defendant was acting maliciously, out of spite or ill will or improper motive. The defence of qualified privilege extends to publication of defamatory statements, providing they were not malicious, if the defamatory statements were made on the following occasions (of which 1 and 4 are likely to be more relevant to doctors):

1   Communications made in the performance or the discharge of a public or private duty, whether legal or moral, to persons who have a like duty or interest in receiving that information

2   Reports of Parliamentary proceedings

3   Fair and accurate reports of judicial hearings if not contemporaneous

4   Communications made for the protection or furtherance of an

interest to persons who have a common or corresponding interest in receiving the same

5   Statutory reports.

Unintentional defamation

This statutory defence of "an offer of amends" was designed to give a defendant protection where there had been a genuine mistake or the innocent misuse of another's name and, in order to establish the defence (under Section 4 of the Defamation Act 1952 now simplified under Sections 2-4 of the Defamation Act 1996) the offer of amends must be made in writing and expressed to be an offer under Section 2 of the 1996 Act and must state whether it is a qualified offer. The offer is to:

1   Make a suitable correction and apology

2   Publish the apology in a manner which is reasonable and practical

3   Pay the aggrieved party such compensation (if any) and such costs as can be agreed or determined to be payable.

For the operation of this defence, it is essential that, the person on whose behalf the offer is made, must not have known that the statement complained of referred to the claimant or was likely to be understood as referring to them or that it was false or defamatory of the claimant.

There are further defences or matters which may also assist a defendant. If a doctor is involved in any action for defamation, legal advice should be taken immediately.

Frequently, doctors feel highly aggrieved if a patient complains about them. At the end of a traumatic Discipline Committee hearing, a doctor may feel that they are vindicated and have demonstrated that the complaint was completely unfounded and false. Consequently, they may consider whether to bring proceedings in defamation. Such a course of action should be entered into with great caution, as the complaint and the discipline hearing will attract qualified privilege and therefore, it will be very hard to prove that the patient did not believe the truth of the complaint. Also, the mental state or anguish of the complainant, at the time that the complaint was made, will often be such as to render it impossible for a jury to satisfy itself as to the requisite malicious intention to defeat privilege. In addition, the defendant may be of inadequate means and be unable to meet any judgement leaving the doctor with a large bill. Libel proceedings are expensive in addition to being time consuming. In any circumstance where doctors feel that they have been libelled, they should take careful specialist legal advice before acting.

Doctors have, from time to time, appeared as claimants in the libel Courts. Over the years, the Courts have established that it can be defamatory to state that a doctor lacks ability, qualifications, knowledge, skill, judgement or efficiency in their professional work. It could clearly be defamatory to say that they have caused the death or illness of a patient due to careless, incompetent or reckless treatment, or that they have shown gross ignorance in their treatment of a patient or have shown unprofessional conduct in the treatment of a case.

Commenting on colleagues

Anxieties are experienced by doctors when they are either asked to comment on a colleague's performance or conduct, or more particularly when they feel that they have no option but to inform an appropriate person or authority about a colleague's professional performance. Doctors will also experience anxiety if they suspect that they could be sued for defamation if no fault is found with the colleague.

The GMC has published advice concerning when to take action and when to remain silent:

- Doctors are frequently asked to express a view about a colleague's professional practice. This may, for example, happen in the course of a medical audit or peer review procedure, or when a doctor is asked to give a reference about a colleague. It may also occur in a less direct and explicit way when a patient seeks a second opinion, specialist advice or an alternative form of treatment. Honest comment is entirely acceptable in such circumstances, provided it is carefully considered and can be justified, that it is offered in good faith and that it is intended to promote the best interests of patients.

- Furthermore it is any doctor's duty, where the circumstances so warrant, to inform an appropriate person or authority about a colleague whose professional performance appears to be in some way deficient. Arrangements exist to deal with such problems, and they must be used in order to ensure that high standards of medical practice are maintained.

- However, gratuitous and unsustainable comment which, whether directly or by implication, sets out to undermine trust in a professional colleague's knowledge or skills, is unethical.

This advice reflects both the nature and needs of professional obligations and also the impact of the law of defamation upon these duties. It emphasises the conflicting demands – demands which are the essence of good professional practice to resolve.

Doctors must recognise, however, that in reporting colleagues in a manner which they themselves may view as a proper discharge of their responsibility, may be viewed by other people concerned as "gratuitous and unsustainable comment". In cases such as these, "off the record comments" are clearly inappropriate. The practical advice must be that, a non-malicious measured statement made to an appropriate person (not to the world at large) after a careful appraisal of the evidence available, will not give grounds for a successful claim of defamation against the person making the statement as they will be protected by qualified privilege.

CHAPTER 9

THE NHS PLAN AND
THE FUTURE

In July 2000 the Secretary of State for Health presented to Parliament the NHS Plan: a plan for investment and reform which set out a 10-year plan for the modernisation of the National Health Service in England.

The plan was supported by all the major bodies involved in the provision of healthcare, including the BMA, and support was given to 10 stated principles:

1   The NHS will provide a universal service for all based on clinical need, not ability to pay.

2   The NHS will provide a comprehensive range of services.

3   The NHS will shape its services round the needs and preferences of individual patients, their families and their carers.

4   The NHS will respond to different needs of different populations.

5   The NHS will work continuously to improve quality services and to minimise errors.

6   The NHS will support and value its staff.

7   Public funds for healthcare will be devoted solely to NHS patients.

8   The NHS will work together with others to ensure a seamless service for patients.

9 The NHS will keep people healthy and work to reduce health inequalities.

10 The NHS will respect the confidentiality of individual patients and provide open access to information about services, treatment and performance.

Clearly substantial funding would be needed to achieve the aims identified in the plan and the Prime Minister in his foreword noted that in March 2000 the Government had made an historic commitment to a sustained increase in NHS spending which over five years would amount to an increase of a third in real terms and which, over time, the Government aims to bring up to the EU average. The commitment was however related to a "deal" whereby the Government would spend the money but only if it also changed chronic system failures of the NHS. Money had to be accompanied by modernisation, investment and reform. Of particular note to GPs was the statement in the Executive Summary that for the first time there would be modern contracts for GPs. There would also be a big extension on quality-based contracts for GPs in general and for single-handed practices in particular.

The Executive Summary also contained a number of aims to insure that, for the first time, patients would have a real say in the NHS. Patients were to have new powers and more influence in the way the NHS works. In particular:

- Letters about an individual patient's care will be copied to the patient

- Better information will be provided to help patients choose a GP, and

- Patients' surveys and forums will help services become more patient-centred.

As to access to medical care, it was stated that by 2004, patients will be able to have a GP appointment within 48 hours and there will be up to 1,000 specialist GPs taking referrals from fellow GPs.

Section 8 of the National Plan dealt with changes for NHS doctors and a number of bold changes were proposed:

- There will be 2,000 more GPs and 450 more GPs in training by 2004. This will be just a start – fast growth in the number of GPs will need to continue beyond 2004.

- There will be a bigger role for GPs in shaping local services as more become specialist GPs, as Primary Care Trusts become universal and as New Care Trusts, incorporating Social Services as well as Health Services, come on stream.

- Pressure on GP services will be eased as nurses and other community staff, together with a new generation of graduate Primary Care Mental Health workers, take on more tasks.

- Up to 3,000 family doctors' premises including 200 new Primary Care Centres will benefit from a £1 billion investment programme by 2004.

- GPs will be helped with their continuing professional development through ear-marked funds, and

- NHS Occupational Health Services will be extended to cover family doctors.

The Personal Medical Services (PMS) type of contract was extolled and it was claimed that by April 2002 the Government expected that nearly a third of all GPs would be working under PMS contracts. It is believed however that this is not a target that will be reached and by April 2002 the figure may well be less than 20%.

Whilst the Core PMS Contract is being developed, the Government additionally gave a commitment to work with GPs and their representatives to amend the National "Red Book" Contract – the revised National Contract reflecting the emphasis on quality and improved outcomes inherent in the Personal Medical Services approach. By 2004 both local and national arrangements are set to operate within a single contractual framework that will meet the key principles and requirements of the modern NHS. As a result of pressures identified in a major survey of GP opinion (carried out in the late spring of 2001) it may well be that a new GP contract is achieved somewhat sooner than 2004.

Single-handed practices were mentioned particularly in the NHS Plan and, although their hard work and commitment was recorded, it was also noted that they do not have the ready support from colleagues enjoyed by GPs in larger practices. The current "Red Book" Contract was said to be a particularly poor mechanism for protecting quality standards in such practices. For this reason it was then proposed that new contractual quality standards would be introduced for single-handed practices and that this would be done either through a negotiated change to the "Red Book" or, if that proved not to be possible, a new National PMS Contract would be introduced.

A number of the legislative proposals set out in the NHS Plan were implemented through the Health and Social Care Act 2001.

In the summer of 2001 the Government elaborated on key proposals from the NHS Plan in the document: *Shifting the Balance of Power within the NHS – Securing Delivery*. Subsequently the National Health Service Reform and Healthcare Professions Bill, to take forward the various proposals which require primary legislation, was introduced in the House of Commons on the 8th November 2001.

Recognising the changes (which may well be made on the passage of the Bill through Parliament) and given the nature of this work, only the shortest summary of the Bills provisions are set out. The Bill provides, *inter alia*:

- For the amendment of the structural framework of the Health Service in England (and separately in Wales) and provides in England for Health Authorities to be renamed as Strategic Health Authorities. It also provides for most of the functions of Health Authorities to be conferred instead on to Primary Care Trusts and for Health Service resources to be allocated directly to PCTs by the Secretary of State.

- For new arrangements aimed at strengthening the Commission for Health Improvement (CHI) and its independence. The CHI was established by the Health Act 1999 to carry out independent reviews of the arrangements for monitoring and improving the quality of healthcare by NHS bodies and other NHS providers. The Bill makes it clear that the definition of "quality" extends to the patient environment.

- For the abolition of Community Health Councils in England and Wales and the Association of Community Health Councils of England and Wales.

- For the creation of an independent "Patients' Forum" for every NHS Trust and PCT in England to perform a role in inspecting, monitoring and representing Patients and the Public.

- For the establishment of the Commission for Patient and Public Involvement in Health to report to the Secretary of State on how such involvement mechanisms are working. The Commission will have responsibilities to co-ordinate Patients' Forums and provide administrative support.

Undoubtedly the legislative and regulatory changes occurring within the NHS will bring considerable changes to the role and work of the

General Practitioner and whilst this chapter can only begin to hint at what is to come, it is certainly hoped that the changes will be introduced at a sensibly controlled pace and in a way which genuinely benefits both patients and doctors through the performance of a practicable and worthwhile contract.

FURTHER READING

The field of law in general practice is vast, and there are many publications covering different aspects of it. This is simply a list of some of those publications that may be more readily available and give further information on different aspects of this book.

General Practitioners' obligations to patients

The Law and General Practice
edited by D. Pickersgill (Radcliffe Medical Press Ltd, 1992)

Medicine, Patients and the Law
Margaret Brazier (Penguin, 1992)

Medical and nursing ethics

Code of Professional Conduct for the Nurse, Midwife and Health Visitor
(UKCC, 1992)

Good Medical Practice
(GMC, May 2000)

Seeking Patients' Consent: The Ethical Consideration
(GMC, November 1998)

Serious Communicable Diseases
(GMC, October 1997)

Confidentiality
(GMC, September 2000)

Maintaining Good Medical Practice
(GMC, July 1998)

Management in Healthcare: The Role of Doctors
(GMC, December 1999)

Consent, confidentiality, medical records and mental health

Guidance in confidentiality towards people under 16 years is issued by the BMA, GPC, HEA, Brook Advisory Centres, Family Planning Association and RCGP. Other recommended sources of information include:

> ### Medical Ethics Today – Its Practice and Philosophy
> *(BMA, 1993)*

Medical negligence

There is a large and increasing literature on this area of law. It includes:

> ### Principles of Medical Law (and Supplements)
> *I. Kennedy & A. Grubb (Oxford University Press, 1998).*
>
> ### Medical Negligence
> *Powers & Harris (Butterworths, 2000)*

Doctors and courts

> ### Legal Aspects of Medical Practice
> *Bernard Knight (Churchill Livingstone, 1992)*

Employment law

The Advisory Conciliation and Arbitration Service (ACAS) has published codes of conduct and a handbook on various aspects of employment law, including, in particular, disciplinary procedures. The Commission for Racial Equality (CRE) and the Equal Opportunities Commission (EOC) publish leaflets in their field, and Trade Unions publish a large amount of guidance in this area. Other publications of interest include:

> ### Butterworths' Employment Law Guide
> *edited by C. Osman (Butterworths, 3rd Edition 2002)*

Harvey on Industrial Relations and Employment Law
(Butterworths)

Information relating to employment matters can also be obtained from the Department of Trade and Industry website at:

www.dti.gov.uk

The NHS Executive Health Circulars are available on the Department of Health website at:

www.doh.gov.uk/coinh.html

Health and safety

The Health and Safety Executive publishes a large amount of guidance in this area. In addition, trade unions publish advice for safety representatives. Among many general texts available are:

Health and Safety at Work Brief
G. Myles (Locksley Press Limited, 2001)

Tolley's Health and Safety at Work Handbook
(Tolley)

General

The BMA and the GMC have published guidance on the various issues/topics discussed in this book.

GPC Guidance is available on the BMA website at
www.bma.org.uk

GMC Guidance is available on the GMC website at
www.gmc-uk.org

USEFUL ADDRESSES

Advisory, Conciliation and Arbitration Service (ACAS)
27 Wilton Street, LONDON, SW1X 7AZ
Tel no: 020 7211 3000
Web Site: www.acas.org.uk

BMA
BMA House
Tavistock Square, LONDON, WC1H 9JP
Tel no: 020 7387 4499
Fax no: 020 7383 6400
Web Site: www.bma.org.uk

Brook Advisory Centres
421 Highgate Studios
53-79 Highgate Road, LONDON, NW5 1TL
Tel no: 020 7284 6040
Fax: 020 7833 8182
Web Site: www.brook.org.uk

Commission for Health Improvement (CHI)
Finsbury Tower
103-105 Bunhill Row, LONDON, EC1Y 8TG
Tel no: 020 7448 9200
Fax: 020 7448 9222
email: information@chi.nhs.uk
Web Site: www.chi.nhs.uk

Coroners Society of England and Wales
c/o Hon Secretary
44 Ormond Avenue, HAMPTON, Middlesex, TW12 2RX
Tel no: 020 8979 6805

Dispensing Doctors' Association
Cornmill
Kirby Mills, KIRKBY MOORSIDE,
North Yorkshire, YO62 6NP
Tel no: 01751 430192
email: cornmill@kirbymills.demon.co.uk
Web Site: www.dispensingdoctor.org

FHS Appeal Authority
30 Victoria Avenue, HARROGATE, N Yorkshire, HG1 5PH
Tel no: 01423 530280
Fax: 01423 522034

General Medical Council
178-202 Great Portland Street, LONDON, W1N 6AE
Tel no: 020 7580 7642
Fax: 020 7915 3641
email: gmc@gmc-uk.org
Web Site: www.gmc-uk.org

Health and Safety Commission
Rose Court
2 Southwark Bridge, LONDON, SE1 9HS
Tel no: 020 7717 6000
Web Site: www.hse.gov.uk

Health and Safety Executive
HSE Information Services
Caerphilly Business Park, CAERPHILLY, CF83 3GG
Fax: 02920 859260
email: hseinformationservices@natbrit.com
Web Site: www.hse.gov.uk

Health Service Commissioner (Ombudsman)
11th Floor, Millbank Tower
Millbank, LONDON, SW1P 4QP
Web Site: www.ombudsman.org.uk

Her Majesty's Stationery Office
Holborn Bookshop
49 High Holborn, LONDON,
Tel no: 020 7873 0011
Web Site: www.hmso.gov.uk

Home Office:
Drugs Branch
Queen Anne's Gate, LONDON, SW1H 9AT
Tel no: 020 7773 3000

Joint Committee on Postgraduate
Training for General Practice
14 Princes Gate
Hyde Park, LONDON, SW7 1PU
Tel no: 020 7581 3232
Web Site: www.jcptgp.org.uk

Medical & Dental Defence Union of Scotland
(MDDUS)
Mackintosh House
120 Blythswood Street, GLASGOW, G2 4EA
Tel no: 0141 221 5858
Fax: 0141 228 1208
Web Site: www.mddus.com

Medical Council on Alcoholism
3 St Andrew's Place, LONDON, NW1 4LB
Tel no: 020 7487 4445
Fax: 020 7935 4479

Medical Defence Union
230 Blackfriars Road, LONDON, SE1 8PJ
Tel no: 020 7202 1500
Fax: 020 7202 1666
email: mdu@the-mdu.com
Web Site: www.the-mdu.co.uk/index.asp

Medical Practices Committee
1st Floor
Eileen House
80-94 Newington Causeway, LONDON,
Tel no: 020 7972 2930
Fax: 020 7972 2985
Web Site: www.open.gov.uk/doh/mpc/mpch.htm

Medical Protection Society
33 Cavendish Square, LONDON, W1G 0PS
Tel no: 020 7399 1300
Fax: 020 7399 1301
email: info@mps.org.uk
Web Site: www.mps.org.uk

National Counselling Service for Sick Doctors
Tel no: 01455 255171
Fax: 020 7935 8601

National Institute for Clinical Excellence (NICE)
11 Strand, LONDON, WC2N 5HR
Tel no: 020 7766 9191
Fax: 020 7766 9123
email: nice@nice.nhs.uk
Web Site: www.nice.org.uk

NHS Confederation
1 Warwick Row, LONDON, SW1E 5ER
Tel no: 020 7959 7272
Fax: 020 7959 7273
email: firstname.lastname@nhsconfed.co.uk
Web Site: www.nhsconfed.net

NHS Executive
Quarry House
Quarry Hill, LEEDS, LS2 7UE
Tel no: 0113 254 6109
Web Site: www.doh.gov.uk/nhs.htm

NHS Executive Eastern
6-12 Capital Drive
Linford Wood, MILTON KEYNES, MK14 6QP
Tel no: 01908 844400
Fax: 01908 844444

NHS Executive London
40 Eastbourne Terrace, LONDON, W2 3QR
Tel no: 020 7725 5300
Fax: 020 7258 0530

NHS Executive North West
930-932 Birchwood Boulevard
Millenium Park, BIRCHWOOD, Warrington, WA3 7QN
Tel no: 01925 704000
Fax: 01925 704100

NHS Executive Northern and Yorkshire
John Snow House
Durham University Science Park, DURHAM, DH1 3YG
Tel no: 0191 301 1300
Fax: 0191 301 1400

NHS Executive South and West
Westward House
Lime Kiln Close, STOKE GIFFORD BS12 6SR,
Tel no: 0117 984 1750
Fax: 0117 984 1751

NHS Executive South East
40 Eastbourne Terrace, LONDON, W2 3QR
Tel no: 020 7725 2500
Fax: 020 7258 3908

NHS Executive Trent
Fulwood House
Old Fulwood Road, SHEFFIELD, S10 3TH
Tel no: 0114 263 0300
Fax: 0114 263 6956

NHS Executive West Midlands
Bartholomew House
142 Hagley Road, BIRMINGHAM, B16 9PA
Tel no: 0121 224 4600
Fax: 0121 224 4601

Public Health Laboratory Service
61 Colindale Avenue, LONDON, NW9 5DF
Tel no: 020 8200 1295
Web Site: www.phls.co.uk

Royal College of General Practitioners
14 Princes Gate
Hyde Park, LONDON, SW7 1PU
Tel no: 020 7581 3232
Fax: 020 7225 3047
email: info@rcgp.org.uk
Web Site: www.rcgp.org.uk

Royal College of Midwives
15 Mansfield Street, LONDON, W1M 0BE
Tel no: 020 7312 3535
Fax: 020 7312 3536
email: info@rcm.org.uk
Web Site: www.rcm.org.uk

GLOSSARY
OF ABBREVIATIONS

ACAS	*Advisory, Conciliation and Arbitration Service*
AHA	*Area Health Authority*
AML	*Additional Maternity Leave*
BMA	*British Medical Association*
CHI	*Committee for Health Improvement*
COSHH	*Control of Substances Hazardous to Health Regulations 1999*
DoH	*Department of Health*
GMC	*General Medical Council*
GMS	*General Medical Services*
GPC	*General Practitions Committee of the BMA*
HA	*Health Authority*
HCHS	*Hospital and Community Health Services*
HSC	*Health and Safety Commission*
HSE	*Health and Safety Executive*
HSWA	*Health and Safety at Work etc Act 1974*
LMC	*Local Medical Committee*
NHS	*National Health Service*
OML	*Ordinary Maternity Leave*
PCT	*Primary Care Trust*
PMS	*Personal Medical Services*
RRA	*Race Relations Act 1976*
SDA	*Sex Discrimination Act 1975*
UKCC	*United Kingdom Central Council for Nursing, Midwifery and Health Visiting*

140

INDEX

Published in the UK by
Magister Consulting Ltd
The Old Rectory
St. Mary's Road
Stone
Dartford
Kent DA9 9AS

Copyright © 2002 Magister Consulting Ltd
Printed in Italy by Fotolito Longo Group

ISBN 1 873839 48 0

A GUIDE TO

LAW IN GENERAL PRACTICE

by

Andrew Lockhart-Mirams, Solicitor